Really Understand Binary

Rex A. Barzee

Cover Photo

The cover photo shows two red-throated bee-eaters (Merops bulocki) photographed in Cameroon by Dr. Krzysztof Blachowiak of Poland. The photo is used with Dr. Blachowiak's permission. You can see more of his excellent photographic work at ibc.lynxeds.com/users/krzysztof-blachowiak

Really Understand Binary

Published by Maia L.L.C.
Idaho, U.S.A.
maiaco.com

ISBN 978-0-9833840-9-0

Contents

Introduction

The **binary number system**, also called base 2, or binary for short, is used by computers to store numbers and to perform arithmetic. Software developers, network analysts, and computer security analysts are just some of the people who really need to understand binary. A software developer needs to understand binary to understand the limitations that a computer has when doing arithmetic and to write code in a way that compensates for those limitations. A network analyst uses binary to divide and configure networks with subnet masks. A security analyst uses binary to understand data encryption and to analyze hacking attacks.

During my time as student, software developer, and professor, I have seen many books that explain binary by simply showing that to convert from the decimal number system (also called base 10) to binary a person can do the following:

1. Repeatedly divide a decimal number by 2, take the quotient, and divide it by 2 until the quotient is 0.
2. Then write the remainders in reverse order, and this is the binary number.

For example, to convert decimal 103 into binary first repeatedly divide 103 and its quotients by 2 until the quotient is 0.

$$
\begin{array}{ccccccc}
51 & 25 & 12 & 6 & 3 & 1 & 0 \\
2\overline{)103} & 2\overline{)51} & 2\overline{)25} & 2\overline{)12} & 2\overline{)6} & 2\overline{)3} & 2\overline{)1} \\
-10 & -4 & -2 & -12 & -6 & -2 & -0 \\
\hline
3 & 11 & 5 & 0 & 0 & 1 & 1 \\
-2 & -10 & -4 \\
\hline
1 & 1 & 1
\end{array}
$$

Then write the remainders in reverse order, and this is the corresponding binary number.

1	1	0	0	1	1	1

However, this is certainly not an explanation of binary but rather a rote process to convert from decimal to binary and doesn't help a student really understand binary. A better way to understand binary is to first review and understand our normal number system, the decimal number system, and then to apply that understanding to binary, which is exactly what this book will do for you.

1
Number Systems

A **number system** is a set of rules for writing numbers. Throughout history people have used many different number systems, including tally marks, Chinese numerals, and Roman numerals. A **positional number** system is a number system where the position of a digit has value. Today most people count and do arithmetic in a positional number system called **base 10**. It is called base 10 because the number system has ten symbols. In most countries and languages today, those ten symbols are the Arabic numerals: 0, 1, 2, 3, 4, 5, 6, 7, 8, 9. Humans probably started counting and doing arithmetic in base 10 because we have ten fingers.

It is possible to count and do arithmetic in other bases. Some ancient communities counted in base 5 and others in base 20, meaning their number system had only five symbols or twenty symbols respectively. Computers count and perform arithmetic in **base 2** because internally computers are composed of millions of tiny two-state electronic circuits. Each circuit may be either off or on, electric current not flowing or flowing. These two states represent two symbols: 0 and 1, so computers use base 2.

A computer professional needs to be able to convert numbers to and from various bases, especially base 2, base 10, and base 16. This chapter teaches you how to count in several different bases and how to convert numbers between those bases.

Counting

When we count in any base, we start at zero and list the symbols in their normal order in the right-most column. After we have listed all the symbols, we add one to the column immediately to the left and start over listing the symbols in the right-most column again. For example, in base 10

we count from 0 to 9,

Base 10
0
1
2
3
4
5
6
7
8

Base 10
9
10
11
12
13
14
15
16
17
18
19
20
21
⋮

then put a 1 in the ten's column and count from 0 to 9 again,

then put a 2 in the ten's column and count from 0 to 9 again, and so on.

Base 2
0
1
10
11
100
101
110
111
1000
1001
1010
1011
1100
1101
1110
1111
⋮

In base 2 we count from 0 to 1,

then put a 1 in the next column to the left and count from 0 to 1 in the right-most column again, then put a 1 in the next column to the left and again count from 00 to 11 in the two right-most columns,

then put a 1 in the next column to the left and count from 000 to 111 in the three right-most columns again, and so on. When counting in base 2, some people find it helpful to imagine a strange car odometer that has only two digits on each wheel: 0 and 1.

One interesting way to check your work when counting in base 2 is to examine each column of numbers. If you counted correctly, in the right-most column the digits will alternate with 0, then 1, then 0, then 1… The second column from the right will alternate with two zeros, then two ones, then two zeros, then two ones… The third column from the right will alternate with four zeros, then four ones, then four zeros, then four ones… And so on.

Table 1 shows how to count in base 10, base 2, and **base 16** (also called **hexadecimal**). Of course, base 10 is the number system that we use every day, base 2 is used by computers; and base 16 is really just a shortcut for writing base 2 numbers as you will see later in this chapter.

Notice that base 10 has of course ten symbols: 0, 1, 2, 3, 4, 5, 6, 7, 8, 9. However, base 2 has only two symbols: 0 and 1, and that is all. When counting in base 2, every time we reach 1 we have no other symbols, so we have to add one to the column to the left and start again at 0.

Base 16 has sixteen symbols: 0, 1, 2, 3, 4, 5, 6, 7, 8, 9, and a, b, c, d, e, f. The inventors of base 16 could have used any symbols after 9, but they chose symbols that they were familiar with: a, b, c, d, e, f. So when counting in base 16, the letters a…f are used as numeric symbols, each with a numeric value. When counting in base 16 it doesn't matter if we use upper case or lower case letters. In other words, in a base 16 number "a" and "A" have the same value.

Base 10 (decimal)	Base 2 (binary)	Base 16 (hexadecimal)
0	0	0
1	1	1
2	10	2
3	11	3
4	100	4
5	101	5
6	110	6
7	111	7
8	1000	8
9	1001	9
10	1010	a
11	1011	b
12	1100	c
13	1101	d
14	1110	e
15	1111	f
16	10000	10
17	10001	11
18	10010	12
19	10011	13
20	10100	14
21	10101	15
22	10110	16
23	10111	17
24	11000	18
25	11001	19
26	11010	1a
27	11011	1b
28	11100	1c
29	11101	1d
30	11110	1e
31	11111	1f
32	100000	20
33	100001	21

Table 1: Counting in three bases: 10, 2, and 16. Base 10 uses ten symbols: 0…9, base 2 uses only two symbols: 0 and 1, and base 16 uses sixteen symbols: 0…9 and a…f.

Positional Number Systems

To convert a number from one base to another base, we must first understand how positional number systems work. A **positional number system** is a number system where each position or column within a number has value. Base 10 (also called decimal) is a positional number system. Consider the base 10 number 3407. We have an intuitive feel for how large this number is, and we take for granted that the number really means 3 thousands plus 4 hundreds plus 0 tens plus 7 ones or in other words, $(3 * 1000) + (4 * 100) + (0 * 10) + (7 * 1)$. The multiplier for each digit is determined by the digit's position. In base 10 the value of each column is always a power of ten: 1, 10, 100, 1000… It is easy to see the positional value of each digit if we place the number in a table with each column labeled with its positional value as shown in examples 1 and 2.

Example 1

3407 in base 10 means $(3 * 1000) + (4 * 100) + (0 * 10) + (7 * 1)$.

10^3	10^2	10^1	10^0
1000	100	10	1
3	4	0	7

$$
\begin{aligned}
= \quad 3 * 1000 &= 3000 \\
4 * 100 &= 400 \\
0 * 10 &= 0 \\
7 * 1 &= \underline{7} \\
& 3407
\end{aligned}
$$

Example 2

7216 in base 10 means $(7 * 1000) + (2 * 100) + (1 * 10) + (6 * 1)$.

10^3	10^2	10^1	10^0
1000	100	10	1
7	2	1	6

$$
\begin{aligned}
= \quad 7 * 1000 &= 7000 \\
2 * 100 &= 200 \\
1 * 10 &= 10 \\
6 * 1 &= \underline{6} \\
& 7216
\end{aligned}
$$

Really Understand Binary

Binary Number Sizes

Each column in a base 10 number is also called a **decimal digit**. The term decimal digit does not refer to one of the symbols 0...9, but instead a column that contains one of those symbols. Likewise, each column in a base 2 number is called a binary digit or a **bit** (BInary digiT = bit). A bit is not the symbol 0 or 1 but instead a column that contains either the symbol 0 or 1. Table 2 contains the names that professionals use for different sizes of binary numbers. Four bits together are called a **nibble**, eight bits are called a **byte**, sixteen bits are called a **half word**, thirty-two bits are called a **word**, and sixty-four bits are called a **long word**.

Name	Size	Notes
bit	a binary digit	A bit is a single column in a binary number that contains either the symbol 0 or 1.
nibble	4 bits	This name is an inside joke: a nibble is half of a byte.
byte	8 bits	
half word	16 bits	
word	32 bits	Unfortunately, a lot of documentation written by Microsoft uses the term "word" to mean 16 bits.
long word	64 bits	Unfortunately, a lot of documentation written by Microsoft uses the term "long word" to mean 32 bits.

Table 2: The names of various binary number sizes.

Converting between Base 2 and Base 10

To convert from any base to base 10, we make a small table where each column is labeled with a number that is a power of the other base. For example to convert from base 2 to base 10, we make a table with each column labeled with a power of 2 like the ones in examples 3 and 4 and place each digit of the base 2 number in one column starting at the right. Then we multiply to get the base 10 value of each digit and add the values together to get the corresponding base 10 number.

Example 3

Convert the binary (base 2) number 01101011 into decimal (base 10). 01101011 in binary means $(0 * 128) + (1 * 64) + (1 * 32) + (0 * 16) + (1 * 8) + (0 * 4) + (1 * 2) + (1 * 1)$.

			Binary						**Decimal**		
2^7	2^6	2^5	2^4	2^3	2^2	2^1	2^0				
128	64	32	16	8	4	2	1				
0	1	1	0	1	0	1	1	=	0 * 128	=	0
									1 * 64	=	64
									1 * 32	=	32
									0 * 16	=	0
									1 * 8	=	8
									0 * 4	=	0
									1 * 2	=	2
									1 * 1	=	1
											107

Example 4

Convert the binary number 10010100 into decimal.

			Binary						**Decimal**		
2^7	2^6	2^5	2^4	2^3	2^2	2^1	2^0				
128	64	32	16	8	4	2	1				
1	0	0	1	0	1	0	0	=	1 * 128	=	128
									0 * 64	=	0
									0 * 32	=	0
									1 * 16	=	16
									0 * 8	=	0
									1 * 4	=	4
									0 * 2	=	0
									0 * 1	=	0
											148

To convert from base 10 to base 2, we use the same table but instead of adding and multiplying as we did in examples 3 and 4, we divide and subtract as shown in example 5.

Example 5

To convert 173 decimal into an 8 bit number, we do the following:

1. Divide 173 by 128. 128 divides fully into 173 one time, so we place a 1 in the 128 column and subtract 128 from 173 which yields 45. In other words, by writing a 1 in the 128 column, we have accounted for 128 of the original 173, so we only have to account for 45 more (173 − 128).
2. Divide 45 by 64. 64 divides fully into 45 zero times, so we place a 0 in the 64 column.
3. Divide 45 by 32. 32 divides fully into 45 one time, so we place a 1 in the 32 column, and subtract 32 from 45 which gives 13.
4. Divide 13 by 16. 16 doesn't divide fully into 13.
5. Divide 13 by 8. 8 divides fully into 13 one time with a remainder of 5, so we place a 1 in the 8 column.
6. Divide 5 by 4. 4 divides fully into 5 one time with a remainder of 1, so we place a 1 in the 4 column.
7. Divide 1 by 2. 2 doesn't divide fully into 1.
8. Divide 1 by 1. 1 divides fully into 1 one time with a remainder of 0, so we place a 1 in the 1 column.
9. We can check our conversion from decimal to binary by converting the binary number to decimal again, and of course, we should get the same decimal number that we started with.

Decimal		Binary								Decimal		
	2^7	2^6	2^5	2^4	2^3	2^2	2^1	2^0				
	128	64	32	16	8	4	2	1				
173 =	1	0	1	0	1	1	0	1	=	1 * 128 =	128
− 128										0 * 64 =	0
45										1 * 32 =	32
− 32										0 * 16 =	0
13										1 * 8 =	8
− 8										1 * 4 =	4
5										0 * 2 =	0
− 4										1 * 1 =	1
1											173
− 1											
0											

Example 6

Convert 104 decimal into an 8 bit number. The process to do this is the same as the previous example.

1. 104 / 128 = 0 remainder 104
2. 104 / 64 = 1 remainder 40
3. 40 / 32 = 1 remainder 8
4. 8 / 16 = 0 remainder 8
5. 8 / 8 = 1 remainder 0
6. 0 / 4 = 0 remainder 0
7. 0 / 2 = 0 remainder 0
8. 0 / 1 = 0 remainder 0
9. Checking our work by converting from binary to decimal we get 104 again.

Decimal	**Binary**								**Decimal**
	2^7	2^6	2^5	2^4	2^3	2^2	2^1	2^0	
	128	64	32	16	8	4	2	1	

$$104 = \boxed{0 \mid 1 \mid 1 \mid 0 \mid 1 \mid 0 \mid 0 \mid 0} = $$

$$
\begin{array}{r}
104 \\
-64 \\
\hline
40 \\
-32 \\
\hline
8 \\
-8 \\
\hline
0
\end{array}
$$

$$
\begin{array}{rcl}
1 * 64 & = & 64 \\
1 * 32 & = & 32 \\
1 * 8 & = & 8 \\
\hline
& & 104
\end{array}
$$

Example 7

Convert 87 decimal into an 8 bit number.

Decimal	**Binary**								**Decimal**
	2^7	2^6	2^5	2^4	2^3	2^2	2^1	2^0	
	128	64	32	16	8	4	2	1	

$$87 = \boxed{0 \mid 1 \mid 0 \mid 1 \mid 0 \mid 1 \mid 1 \mid 1} = $$

$$
\begin{array}{r}
87 \\
-64 \\
\hline
23 \\
-16 \\
\hline
7 \\
-4 \\
\hline
3 \\
-2 \\
\hline
1 \\
-1 \\
\hline
0
\end{array}
$$

$$
\begin{array}{r}
64 \\
16 \\
4 \\
2 \\
+ 1 \\
\hline
87
\end{array}
$$

Converting between Base 2 and Base 16

Base 16, also called hexadecimal, was invented by computer programmers as a shortcut way of writing binary numbers. It is a shortcut because there are sixteen symbols in hexadecimal, and for a 4 bit number there are sixteen possible combinations of 0 and 1. In other words, each symbol in hexadecimal corresponds directly to a unique pattern of four digits in binary. This means to convert between binary and hexadecimal we can write a simple table like Table 3 and look up 4 bit numbers.

To convert any binary number to hexadecimal, do the following:

1. Starting at the right of the binary number, divide the number into groups of four bits. If the left-most group has fewer than four bits, simply add zeros to the left until it has four bits.
2. Look up each 4 bit group (also called a nibble) in Table 3 and write the corresponding hexadecimal symbol.

Base 2 (binary)	Base 16 (hexadecimal)
0000	0
0001	1
0010	2
0011	3
0100	4
0101	5
0110	6
0111	7
1000	8
1001	9
1010	a
1011	b
1100	c
1101	d
1110	e
1111	f

Table 3: A table to convert between binary and hexadecimal. Each pattern of four bits converts directly into a single hexadecimal symbol.

Example 8

Convert the binary number 01101101 into hexadecimal.

Binary		**Hexadecimal**
0110 1101	*=*	*6d*

Example 9

Convert the binary number 10100010011100 into hexadecimal.

Binary		**Hexadecimal**
0010 1000 1001 1100	*=*	*289c*

Example 10

Convert the hexadecimal number 7e3 into binary.

Hexadecimal		**Binary**
7e3	*=*	*0111 1110 0011*

Example 11

Convert the hexadecimal number 60fa into binary.

Hexadecimal		Binary
60fa	=	*0110 0000 1111 1010*

Example 12

Convert the hexadecimal number face into binary.

Hexadecimal		Binary
face	=	*1111 1010 1100 1110*

Example 12 is an inside joke. Some programmers will initialize variables to funny hexadecimal numbers such as feedface which is binary 1111 1110 1110 1101 1111 1010 1100 1110 and decimal 4,277,009,102. Other notable silly hexadecimal numbers are deadbeef, deadc0de, cafebabe, and badfood.

Example 13

HTML colors are a good example of the use of hexadecimal numbers. Within a CSS file, a web designer could specify that text should be blue in any one of these three ways:

```
body { color: blue; }
body { color: rgb(0,0,255); }
body { color: #0000ff; }
```

The first line uses the color name. The second line uses decimal numbers to specify no red, no green, and maximum blue. The last line uses a hexadecimal number to also specify no red, no green, and maximum blue.

Really Understand Binary

Chapter Summary

- A number system is a set of rules for writing numbers.
- A positional number system is a number system where each column of a number has value.
- In base 10 the value of each column is a power of 10: ...1000, 100, 10, 1. In base 2 the value of each column is a power of 2: ...64, 32, 16, 8, 4, 2, 1.
- To convert from base 2 to base 10, label each column of a base 2 number with its power of 2 value, then multiply and add to get the corresponding base 10 number.
- To convert from base 10 to base 2, label each column of a base 2 number with its power of 2 value, then divide and subtract to get the corresponding base 2 number.
- Base 16, also called hexadecimal, is a number system used as a shortcut for writing base 2 numbers because each symbol in base 16 corresponds to a unique pattern of four bits in base 2.
- To convert between base 2 and base 16, make a table that contains all the hexadecimal digits: 0...9 and a...f and the corresponding 4 bit patterns. Then look up the hexadecimal digits or 4 bit patterns that make up a hexadecimal or binary number.

Review Questions

1. Count vertically from 0 to 50 inclusive in decimal, binary, and hexadecimal.
2. Convert the binary number 0110 1010 to hexadecimal and decimal. Show your work.
3. Convert the hexadecimal number 2e to binary and decimal. Show your work.
4. Convert the decimal number 123 to binary and hexadecimal. Show your work.

2
Binary Arithmetic

Computers count and perform arithmetic in base 2 because internally computer chips are composed of millions of tiny two-state electric circuits. Each circuit may be either off or on, electric current not flowing or flowing. These two states represent two digits: 0 and 1, and so computers use base 2. A programmer needs to understand how a computer performs arithmetic, the limitations of that arithmetic, and how to compensate for those limitations within a program. This chapter shows how a computer performs addition and subtraction in base 2.

Decimal Addition

Before learning how a computer performs addition in base 2, let's review base 10 addition. When adding two decimal numbers, we perform the addition one column at a time beginning at the right-most column. If the sum of one column is greater than 9, then we carry a 1 to the next column to the left. For example when adding 76 and 58, we

1. add 6 and 8 in the right-most column
2. write 4 as the sum of the right-most column
3. carry a 1 to the next column to the left
4. add 1, 7, and 5
5. write 3 as the sum
6. carry a 1 to the next column to the left
7. add 1, 0, and 0
8. write 1 as the sum

$$
\begin{array}{r}
1\ \ 1 \\
7\ \ 6 \\
+\ \ 5\ \ 8 \\
\hline
1\ \ 3\ \ 4
\end{array}
$$

Notice that when adding a single column of two decimal numbers and a possible carry from the previous column, the largest possible sum is 19: 1 (carry) + 9 (first number) + 9 (second number). This means when adding a single column of two decimal numbers and a possible carry from the previous column, there are twenty possible sums for that single column: 0…19, and we will never carry more than 1 to the next column.

Binary Addition

In binary addition, just like decimal addition, the computer adds one column at a time beginning with the right-most column. When a sum is larger than 1, the computer carries a 1 to the next column to the left. When adding a single column of two binary numbers and a possible carry from the previous column, there are only four possible binary sums: 0, 1, 10 (decimal 2), and 11 (decimal 3) as shown in Table 4. Table 4 shows all possible combinations of two binary digits and a carry bit. In part a) we see that $0 + 0 = 0$. Part b) shows that $0 + 1 = 1$. Part d) is interesting because it shows that in binary $1 + 1$ is 0 carry the 1, or in other words, in binary $1 + 1 = 10$. Part h) of Table 4 shows that $1 + 1 + 1$ is 1 carry the 1 or in other words, in binary $1 + 1 + 1 = 11$.

	a)	b)	c)	d)	e)	f)	g)	h)
carry					1	1	1	1
first number	0	0	1	1	0	0	1	1
second number	+0	+1	+0	+1	+0	+1	+0	+1
sum	0	1	1	10	1	10	10	11

Table 4: Addition of all possible combinations of two binary digits and a carry bit.

Example 1

Convert decimal 78 and 13 to binary and add them as binary numbers. Then check the binary sum by converting it to decimal and comparing it to the expected decimal sum.

Decimal		128	64	32	16	8	4	2	1		Decimal
carry					1	1					
first number	78 =	0	1	0	0	1	1	1	0		
second number	+ 13 =	0	0	0	0	1	1	0	1		
sum	91	0	1	0	1	1	0	1	1	=	64
											16
											8
											2
											+ 1
											91

Example 2

Convert decimal 87 and 35 to binary and add them as binary numbers. Then check the binary sum by converting it to decimal and comparing it to the expected decimal sum.

Decimal		Binary								Decimal
		128	64	32	16	8	4	2	1	
carry						1	1	1		
first number	87 =	0	1	0	1	0	1	1	1	
second number	+ 35 =	0	0	1	0	0	0	1	1	
sum	122	0	1	1	1	1	0	1	0	= 64

$$
\begin{aligned}
&64 \\
&32 \\
&16 \\
&8 \\
+\,&2 \\
\hline
&122
\end{aligned}
$$

Subtraction Is Difficult

Subtraction is sometimes difficult because borrowing is messy, so most computers perform subtraction by adding a negative number, and so we need to understand how negative numbers are stored in a computer.

Negative Numbers

How should we represent negative numbers in binary? How do we represent a sign (positive or negative) inside a computer? We want a representation scheme that will

- Represent positive and negative integers
- Perform addition and subtraction easily

Such a scheme was developed many years ago. It is called two's complement.

Two's Complement

In the **two's complement** representation the left-most bit is not used to represent a value but instead is used as the **sign bit**. 0 in the sign bit signifies a number is non-negative (zero or positive). 1 in the sign bit signifies a number is negative. To get the two's complement representation for a negative number, convert the corresponding positive number to binary, invert each bit (switch each 0 to 1 and vice versa), and add 1 to the inverted bits.

Example 3

Compute the two's complement representation for −56. To do this, do the following:

1. convert 56 to binary
2. invert each bit (switch each 0 to 1 and each 1 to 0)
3. add 1 to the inverted bits

Decimal				Binary				
	sign	64	32	16	8	4	2	1
56 =	0	0	1	1	1	0	0	0
invert		1	1	0	0	0	1	1	1
+ 1								1
−56 =	1	1	0	0	1	0	0	0

Notice that the addition adds 1 to the inverted bits only. In other words, the original binary number of 56 is not part of the addition. Also, notice that to avoid cluttering this example, the carry bits are not shown even though carrying is done as part of the addition.

Example 4

Compute the two's complement representation for −114. To do this, first convert 114 to binary, invert the bits, then add 1 to the inverted bits. Again, the carry bits from the addition are not shown.

Decimal				Binary				
	sign	64	32	16	8	4	2	1
114 =	0	1	1	1	0	0	1	0
invert		1	0	0	0	1	1	0	1
+ 1								1
−114 =	1	0	0	0	1	1	1	0

Interestingly the two's complement process to convert a positive number to a negative number and to convert a negative number to a positive number is the same: invert the bits and add 1. This means if we are given a negative binary number (recall that it will have a 1 in the sign bit.) we can determine what decimal number it is by first making it a positive binary number (invert the bits and add 1) and then converting that positive binary number to decimal. This positive number will be the opposite of the original negative number.

Example 5

Determine the decimal value of this negative binary number: 10010100. To do this, do the following:

1. Make the binary number positive by inverting its bits and adding 1.
2. Convert that positive binary number to decimal.
3. This positive decimal number will be the opposite of the original negative binary number.

Just as in the two previous examples, the addition involves only the inverted bits and 1. Also, the carry bits from the addition are not shown.

	sign	64	32	16	8	4	2	1	Decimal
	Binary								
	1	0	0	1	0	1	0	0	
invert	0	1	1	0	1	0	1	1	
+ 1								1	
	0	1	1	0	1	1	0	0	= 64
									32
									8
									+ 4
									108

Since the opposite positive number is decimal 108, we know the original negative binary number 10010100 is −108.

Example 6

Determine the decimal value of this negative binary number: 11001010. To do this first make the binary number positive by inverting its bits and adding 1, then convert that positive binary number to decimal. This decimal number will be the opposite of the original negative binary number. Again, the addition involves only the inverted bits and 1, and the carry bits from the addition are not shown.

	Binary								**Decimal**
	sign	**64**	**32**	**16**	**8**	**4**	**2**	**1**	
	1	*1*	*0*	*0*	*1*	*0*	*1*	*0*	
invert	*0*	*0*	*1*	*1*	*0*	*1*	*0*	*1*	
+ 1								*1*	
	0	*0*	*1*	*1*	*0*	*1*	*1*	*0*	= *32*
									16
									4
									+ 2
									54

Since the opposite positive number is decimal 54, we know the original negative binary number is −54.

Negation

This process of inverting the bits and adding 1 to the inverted bits is how the computer negates a number. In other words, if a programmer writes this code:

```
y = -x
```

the computer will retrieve the number in x, invert its bits, add 1 to the inverted bits, and store the sum in y.

Really Understand Binary

Subtracting by Adding

A computer does not perform subtraction by using borrowing as people do. To subtract, a computer simply negates the second number and adds that to the first number. This is possible because $x - y = -y + x$

Example 7

Using the two's complement representation compute $121 - 73$. Then check your work by converting the binary result of $121 - 73$ to decimal and comparing the result to the expected decimal result. In other words, do the following:

1. convert 73 to binary
2. negate binary 73 by inverting its bits and adding 1 to the inverted bits
3. convert 121 to binary
4. add binary -73 to binary 121
5. convert the resulting sum to decimal
6. compare the decimal sum to the expected result of the subtraction

Decimal		sign	64	32	16	8	4	2	1	Decimal	
					Binary					**Decimal**	
73	=	0	1	0	0	1	0	0	1		
invert		1	0	1	1	0	1	1	0		
+ 1									1		
− 73	=	1	0	1	1	0	1	1	1		
121	=	0	1	1	1	1	0	0	1		
sum		0	0	1	1	0	0	0	0	=	32
											+ 16
											48

Notice that the carry bits for the addition are not shown, and that after the left-most column (the sign column) is added there is another 1 to carry to the next column. However, the computer ignores this last carry. Also notice that the binary result of adding $-73 + 121$ is decimal 48 which is the expected result for $121 - 73$.

Example 8

Using the two's complement representation compute 53 – 64. Then check your work by converting the binary result of 53 – 64 to decimal and comparing the decimal result to the expected decimal result. In other words, do the following:

1. convert 64 to binary
2. negate binary 64 by inverting its bits and adding 1 to the inverted bits
3. convert 53 to binary
4. add binary –64 to binary 53
5. convert the resulting sum to decimal
6. compare the decimal sum to the expected result of the subtraction

Decimal		**Binary**							
		sign	**64**	**32**	**16**	**8**	**4**	**2**	**1**
64	=	*0*	*1*	*0*	*0*	*0*	*0*	*0*	*0*
invert		*1*	*0*	*1*	*1*	*1*	*1*	*1*	*1*
+ 1									*1*
–64	=	*1*	*1*	*0*	*0*	*0*	*0*	*0*	*0*
53	=	*0*	*0*	*1*	*1*	*0*	*1*	*0*	*1*
sum		*1*	*1*	*1*	*1*	*0*	*1*	*0*	*1*

Notice that the result of –64 + 53 is negative as we expected. We know it is negative because there is a 1 in the sign bit of the sum in the problem above. We would like to know what negative number this is so we can check our work. To find out what negative number it is, we will negate it (invert its bits and add 1) and convert it to decimal.

	Binary									**Decimal**
	sign	**64**	**32**	**16**	**8**	**4**	**2**	**1**		
sum	*1*	*1*	*1*	*1*	*0*	*1*	*0*	*1*		
invert	*0*	*0*	*0*	*0*	*1*	*0*	*1*	*0*		
+ 1								*1*		
	0	*0*	*0*	*0*	*1*	*0*	*1*	*1*	=	*8*
										2
										+ 1
										11

The result of negating the sum is 11, so the sum of –64 + 53 is –11 which is the answer we expected from 53 – 64.

Subtracting by Adding in Base 10

Interestingly, it is possible to subtract in base 10 by adding the complement of a number in a way similar to the binary method shown in examples 7 and 8. For example, we can compute $74 - 39$ by finding the decimal complement of 39 and adding that to 74. We compute the complement of a base 10 number by

1. inverting the digits by finding the opposite digit for each digit in Table 5
2. adding 1 to the number made up of the opposite digits

For example, the complement of 39 is $60 + 1 = 61$.

Example 9

Compute $74 - 39$ by finding the complement of 39 and adding that complement to 74.

		3	9
invert		6	0
+ 1			1
-39	=	6	1
+		7	4
sum		3	5

Decimal Digit	Opposite Digit
0	9
1	8
2	7
3	6
4	5
5	4
6	3
7	2
8	1
9	0

Table 5: The ten decimal digits and their opposite decimal digit.

Notice that just like the two's complement examples, the carry from the left-most column is ignored. Notice also that adding the complement of 39 (which is 61) to 74 results in 35 (if we ignore the last carry), and 35 is the expected result of $74 - 39$.

Multiplying by Adding

The root of the word multiplication is multiple because multiplication is simply addition done multiple times. In other words, a computer could multiply by adding multiple times. For example to calculate 17 * 5, a computer could calculate 17 + 17 + 17 + 17 + 17. Example 10 contains simple Java code that multiplies by adding multiple times. However, this is a slow way to multiply, and there are shortcuts for multiplying, so in practice computers do not multiply simply by adding multiple times. Some of these shortcuts are shown in the next chapter.

Each of the parts of a multiplication problem has a name: the **multiplicand** is the first number to multiply, the **multiplier** is the second number, and the **product** is the result of the multiplication. In other words, *product = multiplicand * multiplier*.

Example 10

```java
/** Multiplies two numbers: a multiplicand and
 * a multiplier, by adding multiple times. */
public static int multiply(int mcand, int mplier) {

    // Compute the sign of the product.
    boolean negative = (mcand < 0) != (mplier < 0);

    // Make the multiplicand and the multiplier non-negative.
    mcand = Math.abs(mcand);
    mplier = Math.abs(mplier);

    // If the multiplier is larger than the multiplicand,
    // then exchange their values.  We want the multiplier
    // to contain the smaller number so that the while
    // loop below repeats fewer times.
    if (mplier > mcand) {
        int swap = mcand;
        mcand = mplier;
        mplier = swap;
    }

    // Compute the product.
    int prod = 0;
    while (mplier != 0) {
        prod += mcand;
        mplier--;
    }

    // If the product should be negative then negate it.
    if (negative) {
        prod = -prod;
    }

    return prod;
}
```

Dividing by Subtracting

Division is the opposite (or nearly the opposite) of multiplication, so if multiplication can be implemented by adding multiple times, division can be implemented by subtracting multiple times as shown in example 11. However, this chapter already showed that a computer doesn't subtract numbers but rather adds negative numbers. This means that at its core, a computer doesn't have to subtract, multiply, or divide. It simply has to invert bits and add, and all the other mathematical operations can be implemented by inverting and adding.

Each of the parts of a division problem has a name: the **dividend** is the first number in the problem and is divided by a **divisor** which results in a whole number **quotient** and a whole number **remainder**. In other words, *quotient = dividend / divisor* with a *remainder*.

Example 11

```java
/** Divides a dividend by a divisor
 * by subtracting multiple times. */
public static int divide(int dend, int dsor) {
    int quot = 0;
    if (dsor == 0) {
        throw new ArithmeticException("divide by 0");
    }
    else if (dend == 0x80000000 && dsor == -1) {
        throw new ArithmeticException("overflow");
    }
    else {
        // Compute the sign of the quotient.
        boolean negative = (dend < 0) != (dsor < 0);

        // Make the dividend and the divisor non-negative.
        dend = Math.abs(dend);
        dsor = Math.abs(dsor);

        // Compute the quotient.
        while (dend >= dsor) {
            dend -= dsor;
            quot++;
        }

        // If the quotient should be negative then negate it.
        if (negative) {
            quot = -quot;
        }
    }
    return quot;
}
```

Binary Number Ranges

A very important question to ask is, "What is the range of numbers that a computer can store in an 8 bit number?" For example, the range of numbers that a computer can store in an 8 bit unsigned (not two's complement) number is [0, 255] (every integer between 0 and 255, inclusive). Table 6 shows the smallest and largest numbers that can be stored in an 8 bit unsigned number.

The range of numbers that a computer can store in an 8 bit two's complement number is the same size as the range of numbers that can be stored in an 8 bit unsigned number. However, the range is shifted into the negative integers. Table 7 shows the most negative and most positive numbers that can be stored in an 8 bit two's complement number which are −128 and 127 which means the range of numbers that can be stored in an 8 bit two's complement number is [−128, 127].

This means if a programmer wishes to store integers more negative than −128 or larger than 127, the programmer must use 16 bit, 32 bit, 64 bit, or larger two's complement numbers in a program. Table 8 shows the range of numbers that can be stored in 8 bit, 16 bit, 32 bit, and 64 bit two's complement binary numbers. Remember from your math class, that when writing a range of numbers, brackets: [and] mean inclusive and parentheses: (and) mean exclusive.

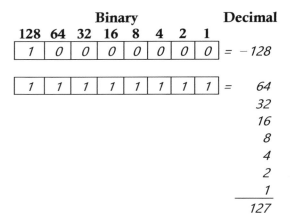

Table 6: The smallest and largest numbers that can be stored in an unsigned 8 bit number: 0 and 255.

Table 7: The smallest and largest numbers that can be stored in a two's complement 8 bit number: −128 and 127.

Some people mistakenly believe that each time we double the number of bits in a binary number that the range also doubles. This is not true. Instead, each time we add a bit, the range doubles. For example, a 9 bit number has twice the range of an 8 bit number, a 10 bit number has four times the range of an 8 bit number, and a 16 bit number has 256 times the range of an 8 bit number because increasing the number of bits from 8 to 16 doubles the range 8 times.

Name	Size	Range		
Byte	8 bits	$[-2^7, 2^7)$	=	$[-128,\ 127]$
short word	16 bits	$[-2^{15}, 2^{15})$	=	$[-32,768,\ 32,767]$
Word	32 bits	$[-2^{31}, 2^{31})$	=	$[-2,147,483,648,\ 2,147,483,647]$
long word	64 bits	$[-2^{63}, 2^{63})$	=	$[-9,223,372,036,854,775,808,$ $9,223,372,036,854,775,807]$
	n bits	$[-2^{n-1}, 2^{n-1})$		

Table 8: The range of numbers that can be stored in various sizes of two's complement binary numbers.

Chapter Summary

- When adding two decimal numbers we start at the right-most column, add one column at a time, and sometimes carry a 1 to the next column to the left.
- Likewise, when adding two binary numbers we start at the right-most column, add one column at a time, and sometimes carry a 1 to the next column to the left.
- Nearly all modern computers use two's complement to store positive and negative numbers. This is because two's complement enables a computer to subtract by adding a negative number.
- To change the sign of a two's complement binary number, simply invert all the bits of the number, and then add 1 to the inverted bits. This will be the same quantity as the original number but with the opposite sign.
- Multiplication could be implemented in a computer by adding multiple times. Division could be implemented by subtracting multiple times.
- Two's complement binary numbers with only 8 bits can store only small numbers in the range of $[-128, 127]$.
- Each time we add another bit to a number, the range of numbers that can be stored doubles.

Review Questions

Perform the following calculations using 8 bit, two's complement, binary arithmetic. Check your answers by converting each binary answer to decimal and comparing it to the expected decimal result. Show your work.

1. $37 + 62$
2. $59 - 29$
3. $73 - 113$
4. $-19 - 42$

3
Bitwise Operators

Recall from chapter 1, that a **bit** is a binary digit or a single column in a binary number. When there is a 0 stored in a bit, we say that bit is off or **clear**. When a 1 is stored in a bit, we say that bit is on or **set**. A **bitwise operation** is a manipulation of one or two binary numbers to produce another binary number. The word "bitwise" in the term bitwise operation reminds us that the value of a bit in the resulting number depends only on the value of the corresponding bits in the input numbers. This is unlike addition, which is an arithmetic operator. The value of a bit after addition depends on the value of the corresponding bits in the input numbers and on the value of the bits in the columns to the right because of a possible carry. In other words, when a computer performs a bitwise operation, each column is independent of the others.

There are seven standard bitwise operations that a computer can perform:

- left shift
- unsigned right shift
- signed right shift
- not
- and
- or
- exclusive or

All seven of them are explained in this chapter. The examples in this chapter are written in Java, but many programming languages have similar bitwise operators. In Java, the data type byte has 8 bits, short has 16 bits, int has 32 bits, and long has 64 bits. Each code example in this chapter has a table below it that shows the value of each variable from the example in decimal, hexadecimal, and binary.

Left Shift

The **left shift** operator is two less than symbols (<<) and shifts all the bits in an integer to the left by a specified number of columns, filling the right-most bits with 0 and losing the values in the left-most bits. For example, $1111 << 2 = 1100$. Arithmetically this is the same as multiplying an integer by a power of two. In other words, if the variable x holds an integer, $x << n$ is equivalent to $x \times 2^n$.

Example 1

```
int x = 58;
int pos = x << 2;   // 58 * 4 = 232
int z = -42;
int neg = z << 2;   // -42 * 4 = -168
```

var	dec	hex	binary
x	58	0000003a	0000 0000 0000 0000 0000 0000 0011 1010
pos	232	000000e8	0000 0000 0000 0000 0000 0000 1110 1000
z	−42	ffffffd6	1111 1111 1111 1111 1111 1111 1101 0110
neg	−168	ffffff58	1111 1111 1111 1111 1111 1111 0101 1000

Unsigned Right Shift

The **unsigned right shift** operator (also called the logical right shift operator) is three greater than symbols (>>>) in the Java programming language and shifts all the bits in an integer to the right by a specified number of columns, filling the left-most bits with 0 and losing the values in the right-most bits. For example, $1111 >>> 2 = 0011$. Arithmetically this is the same as dividing any *non-negative* integer by a power of two. If the variable x holds a non-negative integer, then $x >>> n$ is equivalent to using integer division to compute $x / 2^n$.

Recall that integer division always truncates the quotient to an integer[1]. In other words, integer division simply ignores the remainder. This is what right shift does. It shifts all the bits to the right, losing the right-most bits, which is the same as dividing a non-negative integer by a power of two and ignoring the remainder.

---

[1] There are at least two competing definitions for integer division. In C, C++, Java, and many other languages integer division truncates toward zero. However, in Python, integer division, which is two forward slashes (//), truncates to the previous integer. For simplicity, this book uses the same definition of integer division as C, C++, and Java.

Really Understand Binary

The word "unsigned" in the term `unsigned right shift` reminds us that this operator always produces a non-negative integer. In other words, `unsigned right shift` always loses the sign of the original integer.

Example 2

```
int x = 58;
int pos = x >>> 2;  //  58 / 4 = 14
int z = -42;
int neg = z >>> 2;   // -42 / 4 != 1,073,741,813
```

var	dec	hex	binary
x	58	0000003a	0000 0000 0000 0000 0000 0000 0011 1010
pos	14	0000000e	0000 0000 0000 0000 0000 0000 0000 1110
z	−42	ffffffd6	1111 1111 1111 1111 1111 1111 1101 0110
neg	1073741813	3ffffff5	0011 1111 1111 1111 1111 1111 1111 0101

Notice from example 2 that using `unsigned right shift` to divide a negative integer by a power of two always returns a non-negative integer. This is because `unsigned right shift` places a zero in the sign bit. Therefore, attempting to divide a negative integer by using `unsigned right shift` will always give a wrong answer.

Signed Right Shift

In a two's complement integer, the left-most bit is the sign bit and contains a 0 if the integer is non-negative and contains a 1 if the integer is negative. The **signed right shift** operator (also called the arithmetic right shift operator) is two greater than symbols (>>) and shifts all the bits in an integer to the right by a specified number of columns, filling the left-most bits with the value that was in the sign bit before the operation began and losing the values in the right-most bits. For example, 1011 >> 2 = 1110. Arithmetically this is the same as dividing any *non-negative* integer by a power of two. If the variable x holds a non-negative integer, then `x >> n` is equivalent to using integer division to compute $x / 2^n$.

Example 3

```
int x = 58;
int pos = x >> 2;   // 58 / 4 = 14
int z = -42;
int neg = z >> 2;
```

var	dec	hex	binary
x	58	0000003a	0000 0000 0000 0000 0000 0000 0011 1010
pos	14	0000000e	0000 0000 0000 0000 0000 0000 0000 1110
z	−42	ffffffd6	1111 1111 1111 1111 1111 1111 1101 0110
neg	−11	fffffff5	1111 1111 1111 1111 1111 1111 1111 0101

Because signed right shift preserves the value of the sign bit, it is also the same as dividing any negative integer by a power of two *if* no 1 bits are lost on the right side of the integer when shifting it right. In other words if you use signed right shift to divide negative integers by 2 (x >> 1), the answer will be the same as integer division half the time. If you use signed right shift to divide negative integers by 4 (x >> 2), the answer will be the same as integer division only one fourth of the time, and so on.

Example 4

```
int w = -40;
int ssrw = w >> 2;   // -40 / 4 == -10
int x = -41;
int ssrx = x >> 2;   // -41 / 4 != -11
int y = -42;
int ssry = y >> 2;   // -42 / 4 != -11
int z = -43;
int ssrz = z >> 2;   // -43 / 4 != -11
```

var	dec	hex	binary
w	−40	ffffffd8	1111 1111 1111 1111 1111 1111 1101 1000
ssrw	−10	fffffff6	1111 1111 1111 1111 1111 1111 1111 0110
x	−41	ffffffd7	1111 1111 1111 1111 1111 1111 1101 0111
ssrx	−11	fffffff5	1111 1111 1111 1111 1111 1111 1111 0101
y	−42	ffffffd6	1111 1111 1111 1111 1111 1111 1101 0110
ssry	−11	fffffff5	1111 1111 1111 1111 1111 1111 1111 0101
z	−43	ffffffd5	1111 1111 1111 1111 1111 1111 1101 0101
ssrz	−11	fffffff5	1111 1111 1111 1111 1111 1111 1111 0101

The best way to use right shift with all integers (positive and negative) and to get the same result as integer division by a power of 2 is to add $2^k - 1$ to negative integers before using signed right shift, where k is the number of bits to shift right. The next example demonstrates signed right shift to correctly divide a negative integer by 4.

Example 5

```
int x = -43;
if (x < 0) {
    x += (1 << 2) - 1;  // can be simplified to x += 3;
}
int div = x >> 2;  // -43 / 2 == -10
```

var	dec	hex	binary
x	−43	ffffffd5	1111 1111 1111 1111 1111 1111 1101 0101
x	−40	ffffffd8	1111 1111 1111 1111 1111 1111 1101 1000
div	−10	fffffff6	1111 1111 1111 1111 1111 1111 1111 0110

Not

The **bitwise not** operator is the tilde (~) and takes an integer as input and clears every set bit and sets every clear bit, or in other words, switches every 1 bit to 0 and every 0 bit to 1. For example, ~1011 = 0100. This is the operator that inverts all the bits in a number as described in the *Two's Complement* section of chapter 2.

Example 6

```
short x = 58;
short result = ~x;
```

var	dec	hex	binary
x	58	003a	0000 0000 0011 1010
result	−59	ffc5	1111 1111 1100 0101

And

The **bitwise and** operator is the ampersand (&) and takes two integers as input and produces an integer with bits set where the bits are set in both inputs and clear everywhere else. For example, 0011 & 0101 = 0001. This is the same operation as logical and but performed on each bit. Within a program, bitwise and is often used to test if a bit is set and to clear bits in a variable.

Example 7

```
short x =  58;
short y = 107;
short result = x & y;
```

var	dec	hex	binary
x	58	003a	0000 0000 0011 1010
y	107	006b	0000 0000 0110 1011
result	42	002a	0000 0000 0010 1010

Or

The **bitwise or** operator is the vertical bar (|) and takes two integers as input and produces an integer with bits set where the bits are set in either or both inputs and clear where the input bits are both clear. For example, 0011 | 0101 = 0111. This is the same operation as logical or but performed on each bit. Within a program, bitwise or is often used to set bits in a variable.

Example 8

```
short x =   58;
short y = 107;
short result = x | y;
```

var	dec	hex	binary
x	58	003a	0000 0000 0011 1010
y	107	006b	0000 0000 0110 1011
result	123	007b	0000 0000 0111 1011

Exclusive Or

The **bitwise exclusive or** operator is the caret (^) and takes two integers as input and produces an integer with bits set where the bits in the two inputs are different and clear where the input bits are the same. For example, 0011 ^ 0101 = 0110. This is the same operation as logical exclusive or but performed on each bit. Within a program, bitwise exclusive or is often used in data encryption and can even be used to swap the values of two variables.

Example 9

```
short x =   58;
short y = 107;
short result = x ^ y;
```

var	dec	hex	binary
x	58	003a	0000 0000 0011 1010
y	107	006b	0000 0000 0110 1011
result	94	0051	0000 0000 0101 0001

Shortcut Operators

In many programming languages, all the bitwise operators, except not (~), can be combined with the assignment operator (=) to make shortcut operators as shown in the next example.

Example 10

```
int x = 58;
x &= 0x0f;
x |= 0x70;
x ^= 0xb7;
x <<= 2;
x >>>= 1;
x >>= 1;
```

var	dec	hex	binary
x	58	0000003a	0000 0000 0000 0000 0000 0000 0011 1010
x &= 0x0f	10	0000000a	0000 0000 0000 0000 0000 0000 0000 1010
x |= 0x70	122	0000007a	0000 0000 0000 0000 0000 0000 0111 1010
x ^= 0xb7	205	000000cd	0000 0000 0000 0000 0000 0000 1100 1101
x <<= 2	820	00000334	0000 0000 0000 0000 0000 0011 0011 0100
x >>>= 1	410	0000019a	0000 0000 0000 0000 0000 0001 1001 1010
x >>= 1	205	000000cd	0000 0000 0000 0000 0000 0000 1100 1101

Bitsets

An efficient way to store many Boolean variables is in a single integer where each bit is a Boolean variable with 0 in a bit meaning false and 1 meaning true. An integer or group of integers used in this way is called a **bitset**. The Java code to set, test, and clear bits is shown in the next example.

Example 11

```java
int x = 58;
x |= (1 << 2);  // Turn on bit #2

// Test if bit #2 is turned on
if ((x & (1 << 2)) != 0) {
    System.out.println("bit 2 is set");
}
else {
    System.out.println("bit 2 is clear");
}
x &= ~(1 << 3);  // Turn off bit #3
```

var	dec	hex	binary
x	58	0000003a	0000 0000 0000 0000 0000 0000 0011 1010
1 << 2	4	00000004	0000 0000 0000 0000 0000 0000 0000 0100
x |= (1 << 2)	62	0000003e	0000 0000 0000 0000 0000 0000 0011 1110
x & (1 << 2)	4	00000004	0000 0000 0000 0000 0000 0000 0000 0100
1 << 3	8	00000008	0000 0000 0000 0000 0000 0000 0000 1000
~(1 << 3)	−9	fffffff7	1111 1111 1111 1111 1111 1111 1111 0111
x &= ~(1 << 3)	54	00000036	0000 0000 0000 0000 0000 0000 0011 0110

Swap Values

Occasionally we need to write code to swap or exchange the values of two variables. A simple way to do this is to

1. create a temporary variable
2. copy the value of the first variable to the temporary variable
3. copy the value of the second variable to the first variable
4. copy the value in the temporary variable to the second variable

as shown in this Java code that exchanges the values of the variables x and y. Notice the temporary variable is named *swap*.

```
int x = 58;
int y = -42;

// Exchange the values of x and y.
int swap = x;
x = y;
y = swap;
```

However, there is a way to exchange the values of two variables without using a temporary variable. The values of two variables can be exchanged by using bitwise exclusive or three times as shown in this code example.

Example 12

```
int x = 58;
int y = -42;

// Exchange the values of x and y.
x ^= y;
y ^= x;
x ^= y;
```

var	dec	hex	binary
x	58	0000003a	0000 0000 0000 0000 0000 0000 0011 1010
y	−42	ffffffd6	1111 1111 1111 1111 1111 1111 1101 0110
x ^= y	−20	ffffffec	1111 1111 1111 1111 1111 1111 1110 1100
y ^= x	58	0000003a	0000 0000 0000 0000 0000 0000 0011 1010
x ^= y	−42	ffffffd6	1111 1111 1111 1111 1111 1111 1101 0110

Absolute Value

The simplest way to write code to compute the absolute value of a number x is something like this:

```
// Compute the absolute value of x.
int abs = x;
if (x < 0) {
    abs = -abs;
}
```

or this

```
// Compute the absolute value of x.
int abs = x < 0 ? -x : x;
```

However, both code examples contain a decision and a branch because depending on the value in x, the computer must choose to negate that value or not. Computers often execute code that contains a branch more slowly than code that does not. Using bitwise operators, it is possible to compute the absolute value of a number without using a branch[2].

Example 13

```
int neg = -701;
int pos =  496;

// Compute the absolute value of neg.
int y = neg >> 31;
int abs = (neg + y) ^ y;

// Compute the absolute value of pos.
y = pos >> 31;
abs = (pos + y) ^ y;
```

var	dec	hex	binary
neg	−701	ffffffd43	1111 1111 1111 1111 1111 1101 0100 0011
y	−1	ffffffff	1111 1111 1111 1111 1111 1111 1111 1111
neg + y	−702	ffffffd42	1111 1111 1111 1111 1111 1101 0100 0010
abs	701	000002bd	0000 0000 0000 0000 0000 0010 1011 1101
pos	496	000001f0	0000 0000 0000 0000 0000 0001 1111 0000
y	0	00000000	0000 0000 0000 0000 0000 0000 0000 0000
pos + y	496	000001f0	0000 0000 0000 0000 0000 0001 1111 0000
abs	496	000001f0	0000 0000 0000 0000 0000 0001 1111 0000

---

[2] Warren, *Hacker's Delight*, section 2-4, page 17

Really Understand Binary

Network Mask

A **router** is a computer networking device that routes (sends to another router) packets of data from a source host in its network to the router in the destination host's network. An internet protocol (IP) **network address**, which is simply a large number, has two parts: a network prefix and a host number. The **network prefix** occupies the most significant bits of the address, and is the same for all hosts on the same network. Because a router receives all packets sent from hosts in its network but routes only those packets whose destination network is different from its network, a router must have a fast method to determine if a packet is destined for a host on its network or another network. To determine this, a router uses its own network prefix and the bitwise and operator.

Internet protocol version 4 (IPv4) addresses are written in **dot-decimal notation** which is a group of four bytes in decimal separated by periods. For example 192.168.54.15 is an IPv4 address which can be converted to hexadecimal (c0a8030f) and binary (1100 0000 1010 1000 0000 0011 0000 1111).

The network prefix of a network is written as the first address of the network followed by a slash character (/) and the number of bits in the prefix. For example, 192.168.48.0/20 is the network prefix for the network starting at 192.168.48.0 and having a 20 bit network prefix. The corresponding network prefix mask is a 32 bit number with the 20 most significant bits set to 1 and the remaining 12 bits cleared to 0: (1111 1111 1111 1111 1111 0000 0000 0000). From this mask it is easy to see how many unique addresses are in this network. The network mask has 12 zeros, so there are $2^{12} = 4,096$ unique addresses in this network. However, some of the addresses are reserved and cannot be assigned to a host.

When a router receives a packet, it quickly determines if it needs to route the packet or not by extracting the network prefix from the source address and then extracting the network prefix from the destination address and comparing the two network prefixes. If the two network prefixes are different, the router will route the packet. If the two prefixes are the same, the router will ignore the packet because it does not need to be routed to a different network. Extracting and comparing the network prefixes can be done with the code in the next example.

Example 14

```
// Compute the prefix mask from the prefix length. This
// has to be done once only when the router is configured.
int prefixLen = 20;
int prefixMask = ((1 << prefixLen) - 1) << (32 - prefixLen);

// Get the source and destination addresses from the packet
// header. For this example, I made up the addresses.
int sourceAddr = 0xc0a8360f;   // 192.168.54.15
int destAddr   = 0x4a7d8163;   // 74.125.129.99

// Extract the prefixes for the source and destination
// networks and compare the prefixes. This is the
// code the router must execute for each packet.
int sourcePrefix = sourceAddr & prefixMask;
int destPrefix = destAddr & prefixMask;
if (sourcePrefix != destPrefix) {
    /* Find a route for the packet. */
}
```

var	dot-decimal	hex	binary
prefixLen	20		
prefixMask	255.255.240.0	fffff000	1111 1111 1111 1111 1111 0000 0000 0000
sourceAddr	192.168.54.15	c0a8360f	1100 0000 1010 1000 0011 0110 0000 1111
destAddr	74.125.129.99	4a7d8163	0100 1010 0111 1101 1000 0001 0110 0011
sourcePrefix	192.168.48.0	c0a83000	1100 0000 1010 1000 0011 0000 0000 0000
destPrefix	74.125.128.0	4a7d8000	0100 1010 0111 1101 1000 0000 0000 0000

Faster Multiplication

Each of the parts of a multiplication problem has a name: the **multiplicand** is the first number to multiply, the **multiplier** is the second number, and the **product** is the result of the multiplication. In other words, *product = multiplicand * multiplier*. As discussed in chapter 2, a computer could multiply by adding the multiplicand multiple times. However, adding a number many times consumes lots of compute time, so early programmers developed several shortcuts for performing multiplication in base 2.

To understand these shortcuts let's first review base 10 multiplication. To multiply in base 10 we write the multiplicand, and then we write the multiplier below with the right-most columns aligned. Then we multiply the multiplicand by each column in the multiplier producing one intermediate row for each column in the multiplier. Then we add all the intermediate rows, and this total is the product of the multiplication. For example:

		Decimal				
multiplicand				2	1	4
multiplier	×			1	0	5
		1	0	7	0	
		0	0	0		
+		2	1	4		
product		2	2	4	7	0

Multiplying in parts (one column of the multiplier at a time) is possible because

$$xy = x(y_1 + y_2 + \cdots y_n) = xy_1 + xy_2 + \cdots xy_n$$

if

$$y = (y_1 + y_2 + \cdots y_n)$$

In base 10, we split the multiplier into columns where each column has a value that is a power of 10. For example:

$$214 \times 105 = 214 \times (100 + 0 + 5) = (214 \times 100) + (214 \times 0) + (214 \times 5)$$

Multiplication in binary is like multiplication in decimal but much simpler. It is simpler because each bit in the multiplier contains only a 0 or 1, so calculating the intermediate rows before the summation we multiply by either 0 or 1 which is really simple. For example:

Decimal								sign	64	32	16	8	4	2	1	Decimal
multiplicand 13 =								0	0	0	0	1	1	0	1	
multiplier × 5 =								0	0	0	0	0	1	0	1	
								0	0	0	0	1	1	0	1	
							0	0	0	0	0	0	0	0	0	
						0	0	0	0	1	1	0	1		
					0	0	0	0	0	0	0	0			
				0	0	0	0	0	0	0	0				
			0	0	0	0	0	0	0	0					
		0	0	0	0	0	0	0	0						
+	0	0	0	0	0	0	0	0							
product								0	1	0	0	0	0	0	1	= 65

This works for negative numbers as well.

Decimal								sign	64	32	16	8	4	2	1	Decimal
multiplicand −13 =								1	1	1	1	0	0	1	1	
multiplier × 5 =								0	0	0	0	0	1	0	1	
								1	1	1	1	0	0	1	1	
							0	0	0	0	0	0	0	0	0	
						1	1	1	1	0	0	1	1		
					0	0	0	0	0	0	0	0			
				0	0	0	0	0	0	0	0				
			0	0	0	0	0	0	0	0					
		0	0	0	0	0	0	0	0						
+	0	0	0	0	0	0	0	0							
product								1	0	1	1	1	1	1	1	= −65

When multiplying in binary, each intermediate row is either a multiplication by 0 or 1. In other words, each intermediate row is either a copy of the multiplicand or a row of zeros. For each column in the multiplier that contains a 1, there is an intermediate row that is a copy of the multiplicand shifted to the left. For each column in the multiplier that contains a 0, there is an intermediate row of all zeros shifted to the left.

Stated in another way, the shortcuts for multiplication in base 2 were developed by realizing that the multiplier can be split into powers of 2. Then using algebra, the parts of the multiplication can be rearranged so that the original multiplication is converted into a series of multiplications by powers of 2 and additions. Consider 23×11:

$$
\begin{aligned}
23 \times 11 &= 23 \times (8 + 2 + 1) \\
&= 23 \times (2^3 + 2^1 + 2^0) \\
&= (23 \times 2^3) + (23 \times 2^1) + (23 \times 2^0)
\end{aligned}
$$

From the *Left Shift* section of this chapter, we learned that $x \times 2^n$ is equivalent to $x << n$; for example: $23 \times 2^3 = 23 << 3$. This means that a computer can perform multiplication with a series of left shifts and additions. For example, a computer could compute 23×11 by adding 23 eleven times or it could add $(23 << 3) + (23 << 1) + 23$. This shift and add method for multiplying is almost always faster than simply adding multiple times. The algorithm for shift and add multiplication is

1. repeatedly split a multiplier into powers of 2,
2. use left shift to multiply the multiplicand by those powers of 2, and
3. add those intermediate products to get the final product.

Returning to the example of 23×11:

$$
\begin{aligned}
23 \times 11 &= 23 \times (8 + 2 + 1) &&\text{Split the multiplier into powers of 2.} \\
&= 23 \times (2^3 + 2^1 + 2^0) \\
&= (23 \times 2^3) + (23 \times 2^1) + (23 \times 2^0) &&\text{Rearrange the order of the operators.} \\
&= (23 \ll 3) + (23 \ll 1) + 23 &&\text{Use left shift to multiply the} \\
& &&\text{multiplicand by each power of 2.} \\
&= 184 + 46 + 23 &&\text{Add the intermediate products.} \\
&= 253
\end{aligned}
$$

Here is Java code that performs multiplication by repeatedly shifting and adding.

Example 15

```java
/** Multiplies two numbers by repeatedly shifting and adding. */
public static int mult(int mcand, int mplier) {
    // Compute the sign of the product.
    int cs = mcand >> 31;
    int ps = mplier >> 31;
    int sign = cs ^ ps;

    // Make the multiplicand and
    // the multiplier non-negative.
    mcand = (mcand + cs) ^ cs;
    mplier = (mplier + ps) ^ ps;

    // If the multiplicand is smaller than the multiplier,
    // then exchange their values.  We want the multiplier
    // to contain the smaller number so that the while
    // loop below repeats fewer times.
    if (mplier > mcand) {
        mplier ^= mcand;
        mcand ^= mplier;
        mplier ^= mcand;
    }

    // Multiply by using the "shift and add" algorithm.
    int prod = 0;
    while (mplier != 0) {
        int bit = mplier & 1;
        if (bit != 0) {
            prod += mcand;
        }
        mcand <<= 1;
        mplier >>>= 1;
    }

    // If the product should be negative then negate it.
    if (sign != 0) {
        prod = -prod;
    }

    return prod;
}
```

var	dec	hex	binary
mcand	11	0000000b	0000 0000 0000 0000 0000 0000 0000 1011
mplier	−23	fffffffe9	1111 1111 1111 1111 1111 1111 1110 1001
cs	0	00000000	0000 0000 0000 0000 0000 0000 0000 0000
ps	−1	ffffffff	1111 1111 1111 1111 1111 1111 1111 1111
sign	−1	ffffffff	1111 1111 1111 1111 1111 1111 1111 1111
mcand	11	0000000b	0000 0000 0000 0000 0000 0000 0000 1011
mplier	23	00000017	0000 0000 0000 0000 0000 0000 0001 0111

var	dec	hex	binary
mplier	28	0000001c	0000 0000 0000 0000 0000 0000 0001 1100
mcand	23	00000017	0000 0000 0000 0000 0000 0000 0001 0111
mplier	11	0000000b	0000 0000 0000 0000 0000 0000 0000 1011
prod	0	00000000	0000 0000 0000 0000 0000 0000 0000 0000
bit	1		
prod	23	00000017	0000 0000 0000 0000 0000 0000 0001 0111
mcand	46	0000002e	0000 0000 0000 0000 0000 0000 0010 1110
mplier	5	00000005	0000 0000 0000 0000 0000 0000 0000 0101
bit	1		
prod	69	00000045	0000 0000 0000 0000 0000 0000 0100 0101
mcand	92	0000005c	0000 0000 0000 0000 0000 0000 0101 1100
mplier	2	00000002	0000 0000 0000 0000 0000 0000 0000 0010
bit	0		
prod	69	00000045	0000 0000 0000 0000 0000 0000 0100 0101
mcand	184	000000b8	0000 0000 0000 0000 0000 0000 1011 1000
mplier	1	00000001	0000 0000 0000 0000 0000 0000 0000 0001
bit	1		
prod	253	000000fd	0000 0000 0000 0000 0000 0000 1111 1101
mcand	368	00000170	0000 0000 0000 0000 0000 0001 0111 0000
mplier	0	00000000	0000 0000 0000 0000 0000 0000 0000 0000
prod	−253	ffffff03	1111 1111 1111 1111 1111 1111 0000 0011

Adding with Bitwise Operators

In chapter 2 we learned that if we use the two's complement binary representation, then we can subtract by adding negative numbers. Interestingly addition can be performed with three bitwise operators: exclusive or, and, left shift. This means an extremely simple computer could be built that doesn't have any built-in arithmetic operators. Instead, the computer could have the seven bitwise operators: left shift, unsigned right shift, signed right shift, not, and, or, exclusive or; and all the arithmetic operators could be functions that use the bitwise operators. Example 16 shows Java code that adds two numbers using three bitwise operators: exclusive or, and, left shift.

Example 16

```
/** Adds two numbers by using the bitwise operators ^, &, << */
public static int add(int x, int y) {
    int sum = x ^ y;
    int carry = x & y;
    while (carry != 0) {
        x = sum;
        y = carry << 1;
        sum = x ^ y;
        carry = x & y;
    }
    return sum;
}
```

var	dec	hex	binary
x	46	0000002e	0000 0000 0000 0000 0000 0000 0010 1110
y	24	00000018	0000 0000 0000 0000 0000 0000 0001 1000
sum	54	00000036	0000 0000 0000 0000 0000 0000 0011 0110
carry	8	00000008	0000 0000 0000 0000 0000 0000 0000 1000
x	54	00000036	0000 0000 0000 0000 0000 0000 0011 0110
y	16	00000010	0000 0000 0000 0000 0000 0000 0001 0000
sum	38	00000026	0000 0000 0000 0000 0000 0000 0010 0110
carry	16	00000010	0000 0000 0000 0000 0000 0000 0001 0000
x	38	00000026	0000 0000 0000 0000 0000 0000 0010 0110
y	32	00000020	0000 0000 0000 0000 0000 0000 0010 0000
sum	6	00000006	0000 0000 0000 0000 0000 0000 0000 0110
carry	32	00000020	0000 0000 0000 0000 0000 0000 0010 0000
x	6	00000006	0000 0000 0000 0000 0000 0000 0000 0110
y	64	00000040	0000 0000 0000 0000 0000 0000 0100 0000
sum	70	00000046	0000 0000 0000 0000 0000 0000 0100 0110
carry	0	00000000	0000 0000 0000 0000 0000 0000 0000 0000

Encryption

One way to encrypt a message is to combine the message with a random number using `bitwise exclusive or`. A message that is not encrypted is called the **plain text**. The random number is called the **key** and must be as long as the plain text message. An encrypted message is called the **cipher text** and is sent over an unsecure channel from one party to another party. Using this type of encryption, which is called a **one-time pad**, the second party must use the same key to decrypt the cipher text as the first party used to encrypt it. This means that the two parties must have agreed on the key before sending the message, and in order for the encryption to be secure, the key must remain a secret between the two parties and not be shared with anyone else.

Example 17

Encrypt and then decrypt the word "superb" using the hexadecimal number 36a1804be2f359e1 as the key.

```
// Encrypt the word "superb".
long plain = 0x0000737570657262L;  // ASCII values for "superb"
long key = 0x36a1804be2f359e1L;
long cipher = plain ^ key;    // encrypt

// The cipher text would be sent to a second party who
// would receive it and decrypt it using the same key.

long message = cipher ^ key;  // decrypt
```

var	hex	binary
plain	00007375 70657262	0000 0000 0000 0000 0111 0011 0111 0101 0111 0000 0110 0101 0111 0010 0110 0010
key	36a1804b e2f359e1	0011 0110 1010 0001 1000 0000 0100 1011 1110 0010 1111 0011 0101 1001 1110 0001
cipher	36a1f33e 92962b83	0011 0110 1010 0001 1111 0011 0011 1110 1001 0010 1001 0110 0010 1011 1000 0011
message	00007375 70657262	0000 0000 0000 0000 0111 0011 0111 0101 0111 0000 0110 0101 0111 0010 0110 0010

Chapter Summary

- A bitwise operator processes one or two binary numbers and produces another binary number. The value of each bit in the result of a bitwise operator is dependent only on the corresponding bits in the input numbers and is independent of the bits in the other columns.
- There are seven standard bitwise operations: left shift, unsigned right shift, signed right shift, not, and, or, exclusive or.
- Left shift shifts all the bits in an integer to the left by a specified number of columns, filling the right-most columns with zeros: 1111 << 2 = 1100.
- Unsigned right shift shifts all the bits in an integer to the right by a specified number of columns, filling the left-most columns with zeros: 1111 >>> 2 = 0011.
- Signed right shift shifts all the bits in an integer to the right by a specified number of columns, filling the left-most columns with the value that was in the sign bit before the operation began: 1011 >> 2 = 1110.
- Bitwise not switches every 0 to a 1 and vice versa: ~1011 = 0100.
- Bitwise and takes two integers as input and produces an integer with bits set where the bits are set in both inputs and clear everywhere else: 0011 & 0101 = 0001.
- Bitwise or takes two integers as input and produces an integer with bits set where the bits are set in either or both inputs and clear where both input bits are clear: 0011 | 0101 = 0111.
- Bitwise exclusive or takes two integers as input and produces an integer with bits set where the input bits are different and clear where the input bits are the same: 0011 ^ 0101 = 0110.
- In many programming languages the bitwise operators can be combined with the assignment operator to make shortcut operators, such as: &= |= ^= <<= >>>= >>=
- A bitset is an integer used as a group of Boolean variables where each Boolean variable is stored in a single bit.
- It is possible to use the bitwise exclusive or operator to exchange the value in two variables without using a temporary variable.
- Using signed right shift, addition, and bitwise exclusive or, it is possible to compute the absolute value of an integer without using an if statement.
- An IP router uses a network mask and the bitwise and operator to determine if a packet should stay on the local network or be routed to another network.
- A computer can multiply two integers by performing a series of shift and add operations.
- A computer can encrypt and decrypt data with a large random secret key called a one-time pad and the bitwise exclusive or operator.

Review Questions

1. Compute 37 ^ 62 in binary. In other words, convert 37 and 62 to binary and combine them using bitwise exclusive or.
2. Compute 19 | (1 << 3) in binary.
3. Compute 59 & ~(1 << 3) in binary.
4. Compute 58 & (58 − 1) in binary.

4
Real Numbers

Chapters 1—3 showed how a computer performs calculations with integers, but how does a computer process **real numbers**, numbers with a fractional part such as 25.3? Let's first review how real numbers work in base 10.

Base 10 Real Numbers

In a base 10 real number, we use a period[3] to separate the whole digits from the fractional digits, for example 25.3. Just as each column in the whole part (before the period) has a value, each column in the fractional part (after the period) also has a value. However, the values of the columns after the period are always 1 divided by a power of 10 as shown in example 1.

Example 1

10^3	10^2	10^1	10^0	.	10^{-1}	10^{-2}	10^{-3}
1000	100	10	1	.	1/10	1/100	1/1000
7	2	0	5	.	4	0	8

$$
\begin{aligned}
&= 7 * 1000 &&= 7000\ . \\
&\ 2 * 100 &&= 200\ . \\
&\ 0 * 10 &&= 0\ . \\
&\ 5 * 1 &&= 5\ . \\
&\ 4 / 10 &&= .\ 4 \\
&\ 0 / 100 &&= .\ 00 \\
&+\ 8 / 1000 &&= .\ 008 \\
\hline
&&& 7205\ .\ 408
\end{aligned}
$$

---

[3] In many countries, especially European countries, people use a comma instead of a period to separate the whole part from the fractional part of a real number. For example what would be written as 25.3 in the United States would be written as 25,3 in many other countries.

Base 2 Real Numbers

Real numbers in base 2 are similar to real numbers in base 10. However, the values of the columns are always powers of 2 as shown in example 2.

Example 2

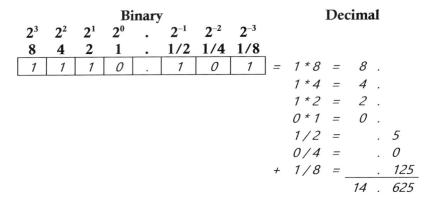

To store a real number a computer could store two binary integers: one for the whole digits and one for the fractional digits. This is how a real number is stored in Java using objects of the BigDecimal class, except the whole part will often grow to be many integers stored in an array instead of just one integer, and the factional part will also often grow to many integers stored in an array.

Really Understand Binary

Adding Real Numbers

When storing a real number with the whole and fractional parts separated, a computer can add real numbers exactly as shown in chapter 2, except the carry bit from adding the fractional bits must be carried into adding the whole bits. For example, here is how a computer could calculate 75.25 + 15.875.

Example 3

Decimal		**sign**	**64**	**32**	**16**	**8**	**4**	**2**	**1**	**.**	**1/2**	**1/4**	**1/8**		**Decimal**		
carry					1	1	1	1	1		1						
75.250	=	0	1	0	0	1	0	1	1	.	0	1	0				
+ 15.875	=	0	0	0	0	1	1	1	1	.	1	1	1				
91.125	=	0	1	0	1	1	0	1	1	.	0	0	1	=	64	.	
															16	.	
															8	.	
															2	.	
															1	.	
														+		.	125
															91	.	125

Scientific Notation

One disadvantage of storing real numbers with separate integers for the whole and fractional parts is that the numbers may occupy a large amount of the computer's memory. Consider the decimal number 20,971,520,000,000,000,000,000. It requires ten bytes to store as an integer, but notice that it has sixteen zeros on its right side. For years, scientists have written such numbers using **scientific notation**, which makes the numbers occupy less space on a page and makes it easier to compare them. A number in scientific notation is written in this form: *significand* $\times 10^{exponent}$, where the **significand** is a real number with only one digit before the period and the **exponent** is an integer. The number 20,971,520,000,000,000,000,000 would be written in scientific notation as: 2.097152×10^{22}.

We can write and store binary numbers in a type of scientific notation as well. The advantage of doing this is that large numbers and very small (very close to zero) numbers will require less space in the computer's memory. The disadvantage is that the numbers may be less precise or in the words of scientists have fewer significant digits.

Floating Point Numbers

Floating point is a method to store approximations of real numbers that is a little like scientific notation. Similar to scientific notation, a floating point number has a significand and an exponent. With floating point we lose precision but gain the ability to store very large and very small (very close to zero) numbers in less memory space. There are several different floating point standards that computers use. However, the most commonly used floating point standard is called **IEEE 754**. IEEE 754 defines several different formats for storing real numbers, including several binary floating point formats: binary16, binary32, binary64, and binary128. Let's examine the **binary32 format** sometimes called **single precision** floating point format.

A computer that uses IEEE 754 binary32 format stores a real number in 32 bits (4 bytes). The bits are laid out as shown in Table 9. The left-most bit (bit 31) is the **sign bit** and has nearly the same meaning as in a two's complement integer: 0 means positive and 1 means negative. The next 8 bits (bit 30—bit 23) are the **exponent**. The last 23 bits (bit 22—bit 0) are called the **fraction** because they are only a fraction (a part) of the significand of the real number. The IEEE 754 standard states that the significand always starts with a 1 bit, so the first bit of the significand is not stored in the fraction because it is always a 1. This means the true significand is a 1 followed by the 23 bits of the fraction.

sign	exponent								fraction																						
0	1	1	0	0	1	0	0	1	0	0	0	1	1	1	0	0	0	0	1	1	0	1	1	1	1	0	0	1	0	1	0
31	30							23	22																						0

Table 9: The layout of bits in the IEEE 754 binary32 format (also called single precision format).

Converting a Floating Point Number to Decimal

To convert an IEEE binary32 floating point number to decimal, use this formula:

$$v = (-1)^s \left(1 + \sum_{1}^{23} b_{23-i} 2^{-i} \right) 2^{e-127}$$

where v is the decimal value, s is the sign bit, b is the bits of the fraction, and e is the exponent.

Example 4

The parts of the binary32 number shown in Table 9 are:

$sign\ bit = 0$

$$
\begin{aligned}
exponent &= 1100\ 1001 \\
&= (1)128 + (1)64 + (0)32 + (0)16 + (1)8 + (0)4 + (0)2 + (1)1 \\
&= 201
\end{aligned}
$$

$$
\begin{aligned}
fraction &= 000\ 1110\ 0001\ 1011\ 1100\ 1010 \\
&= (0)2^{-1} + (0)2^{-2} + (0)2^{-3} + (1)2^{-4} + (1)2^{-5} + (1)2^{-6} + (0)2^{-7} + (0)2^{-8} \\
&\quad + (0)2^{-9} + (0)2^{-10} + (1)2^{-11} + (1)2^{-12} + (0)2^{-13} + (1)2^{-14} \\
&\quad + (1)2^{-15} + (1)2^{-16} + (1)2^{-17} + (0)2^{-18} + (0)2^{-19} + (1)2^{-20} \\
&\quad + (0)2^{-21} + (1)2^{-22} + (0)2^{-23}
\end{aligned}
$$

$$
\begin{aligned}
&= \frac{1}{16} + \frac{1}{32} + \frac{1}{64} + \frac{1}{2048} + \frac{1}{4096} + \frac{1}{16384} + \frac{1}{32768} + \frac{1}{65536} + \frac{1}{1311072} \\
&\quad + \frac{1}{1048576} + \frac{1}{4194304}
\end{aligned}
$$

$$= \frac{462309}{4194304}$$

$$= 0.110223055$$

$$
\begin{aligned}
value &= (-1)^0 \, (1 + 0.110223055) \, 2^{201-127} \\
&= 1.110223055 \times 2^{74} \\
&= 2.097152 \times 10^{22}
\end{aligned}
$$

Example 5

What is the value of the binary32 number: 1 10001011 11000100000000000000000?

$sign\ bit = 1$

$$
\begin{aligned}
exponent &= 1000\ 1011 \\
&= (1)128 + (1)8 + (1)2 + (1)1 \\
&= 139
\end{aligned}
$$

$$
\begin{aligned}
fraction &= 110\ 0010\ 0000\ 0000\ 0000\ 0000 \\
&= (1)2^{-1} + (1)2^{-2} + (1)2^{-6} \\
&= \frac{1}{2} + \frac{1}{4} + \frac{1}{64} \\
&= \frac{49}{64} \\
&= 0.765625
\end{aligned}
$$

$$
\begin{aligned}
value &= (-1)^1 (1 + 0.765625)\ 2^{139-127} \\
&= -1.765625 \times 2^{12} \\
&= -7232
\end{aligned}
$$

Example 6

What is the value of the binary32 number: 0 00010100 00001100110100100000000?

$sign\ bit = 0$

$$
\begin{aligned}
exponent &= 0001\ 0100 \\
&= (1)16 + (1)4 \\
&= 20
\end{aligned}
$$

$$
\begin{aligned}
fraction &= 000\ 0110\ 0110\ 1001\ 0000\ 0000 \\
&= (1)2^{-5} + (1)2^{-6} + (1)2^{-9} + (1)2^{-10} + (1)2^{-12} + (1)2^{-15} \\
&= \frac{1}{32} + \frac{1}{64} + \frac{1}{512} + \frac{1}{1024} + \frac{1}{4096} + \frac{1}{32768} \\
&= \frac{1641}{32768} \\
&= 0.050079346
\end{aligned}
$$

$$
\begin{aligned}
value &= (-1)^0 (1 + 0.050079346)\ 2^{20-127} \\
&= 1.050079346 \times 2^{-107} \\
&= 6.4716136 \times 10^{-33}
\end{aligned}
$$

Really Understand Binary

Converting a Decimal Number to Floating Point

To convert a decimal real number to a binary32 floating point number, do the following:

1. If the real number is negative, the sign bit of the binary32 number is 1, otherwise the sign bit is 0.
2. Convert the whole number part of the real number to binary.
3. Convert the fractional part of the real number to binary for $24 - n$ bits, where n is the number of bits in the converted whole part from step 2.
4. The significand is all the bits from the whole and the fractional parts.
5. The fraction of the binary32 number is the significand with the first bit dropped.
6. The exponent of the binary32 number is $n - 1 + bias$, where n is the number of bits in the converted whole part from step 2 and the *bias* is 127 for binary32.
7. To make the binary32 number, combine the sign bit, exponent, and fraction in that order.

Example 7

Convert the decimal real number -7604.32 to a binary32 floating point number. This binary32 floating point number will be an approximation to -7604.32. Convert the binary32 floating point number back to decimal to see how close the approximation is.

$decimal\ real\ number = -7604.32$

$sign\ bit = 1$

$whole\ part = 7604$
$$= (1)4096 + (1)2048 + (1)1024 + (0)512 + (1)256 + (1)128 + (0)64$$
$$+ (1)32 + (1)16 + (0)8 + (1)4 + (0)2 + (0)1$$
$$= 1110\ 1101\ 1010\ 0$$

$fractional\ part = 0.32$
$$= (0)2^{-1} + (1)2^{-2} + (0)2^{-3} + (1)2^{-4} + (0)2^{-5} + (0)2^{-6} + (0)2^{-7}$$
$$+ (1)2^{-8} + (1)2^{-9} + (1)2^{-10} + (1)2^{-11}$$
$$= 010\ 1000\ 1111$$

$significand = 1110\ 1101\ 1010\ 0010\ 1000\ 1111$

$fraction = 110\ 1101\ 1010\ 0010\ 1000\ 1111$

$exponent = 13 - 1 + 127$
$$= 139$$
$$= (1)128 + (0)64 + (0)32 + (0)16 + (1)8 + (0)4 + (1)2 + (1)1$$
$$= 1000\ 1011$$

$binary32\ number = 1\ 10001011\ 11011011010001010001111$

Now convert 1 10001011 11011011010001010001111 to decimal to see how close it is to −7604.32.

$sign\ bit = 1$

$exponent = 1000\ 1011$
$= (1)128 + (1)8 + (1)2 + (1)1$
$= 139$

$fraction = 110\ 1101\ 1010\ 0010\ 1000\ 1111$
$= (1)2^{-1} + (1)2^{-2} + (1)2^{-4} + (1)2^{-5} + (1)2^{-7} + (1)2^{-8} + (1)2^{-10}$
$+ (1)2^{-14} + (1)2^{-16} + (1)2^{-20} + (1)2^{-21} + (1)2^{-22} + (1)2^{-23}$
$= \dfrac{1}{2} + \dfrac{1}{4} + \dfrac{1}{16} + \dfrac{1}{32} + \dfrac{1}{128} + \dfrac{1}{256} + \dfrac{1}{1024} + \dfrac{1}{16384} + \dfrac{1}{65536} + \dfrac{1}{1048576}$
$+ \dfrac{1}{2097152} + \dfrac{1}{4194304} + \dfrac{1}{8388608}$
$= \dfrac{7185039}{8388608}$
$= 0.85652339458465576171875$

$value = (-1)^1 \times (1 + 0.85652339458465576171875) \times 2^{139-127}$
$= -1.85652339458465576171875 \times 2^{12}$
$= -7604.31982421875$

Notice that we converted the decimal real number −7604.32 to an IEEE binary32 floating point number: 1 10001011 11011011010001010001111. Then we converted that binary32 number back to decimal: −7604.31982421875. The two decimal numbers are not the same, which means the binary32 floating point number is an approximation to the original decimal real number of −7604.32. This is the case with most decimal real numbers. Most decimal real numbers are approximated when stored in a floating point number.

Example 8

Convert the decimal integer 63084 to a binary32 floating point number. Then convert the binary32 number back to decimal to see how close of an approximation the binary32 number is to the original decimal integer.

$sign\ bit = 0$
$whole\ part = 6304$
$\qquad\qquad = (1)32768 + (1)16384 + (1)8192 + (1)4096 + (0)2048 + (1)1024$
$\qquad\qquad\quad + (1)512 + (0)256 + (0)128 + (1)64 + (1)32 + (0)16 + (1)8 + (1)4$
$\qquad\qquad\quad + (0)2 + (0)1$
$\qquad\qquad = 1111\ 0110\ 0110\ 1100$
$fractional\ part = 0$
$\qquad\qquad = 0000\ 0000$

$significand = 1111\ 0110\ 0110\ 1100\ 0000\ 0000$
$fraction = 111\ 0110\ 0110\ 1100\ 0000\ 0000$
$exponent = 16 - 1 + 127$
$\qquad\qquad = 142$
$\qquad\qquad = (1)128 + (0)64 + (0)32 + (0)16 + (1)8 + (1)4 + (1)2 + (0)1$
$\qquad\qquad = 1000\ 1110$
$binary32\ number = 0\ 10001110\ 11101100110110000000000$

Now convert 0 10001110 11101100110110000000000 to decimal to see how close it is to 63084.

$sign\ bit = 0$
$exponent = 1000\ 1110$
$\qquad\qquad = (1)128 + (1)8 + (1)4 + (1)2$
$\qquad\qquad = 142$
$fraction = 111\ 0110\ 0110\ 1100\ 0000\ 0000$
$\qquad\qquad = (1)2^{-1} + (1)2^{-2} + (1)2^{-3} + (1)2^{-5} + (1)2^{-6} + (1)2^{-9} + (1)2^{-10}$
$\qquad\qquad\quad + (1)2^{-12} + (1)2^{-13}$
$\qquad\qquad = \dfrac{1}{2} + \dfrac{1}{4} + \dfrac{1}{8} + \dfrac{1}{32} + \dfrac{1}{64} + \dfrac{1}{512} + \dfrac{1}{1024} + \dfrac{1}{4096} + \dfrac{1}{8192}$
$\qquad\qquad = \dfrac{7579}{8192}$
$\qquad\qquad = 0.9251708984375$
$value = (-1)^0 \times (1 + 0.9251708984375) \times 2^{142-127}$
$\qquad\quad = 1.9251708984375 \times 2^{15}$
$\qquad\quad = 63084$

Notice that we converted the decimal real number 63084 to an IEEE binary32 floating point number: 0 10001110 11101100110110000000000. Then we converted that binary32 number back to decimal: 63084. The two decimal numbers are exactly the same which means the binary32 floating point number is not an approximation but is an exact representation of the original decimal real number of 63084. This is the case with many decimal integers. In fact, all decimal integers between −16,777,216 and 16,777,216 inclusive can be stored exactly in a binary32 floating point number as shown in Table 13. All integers not within that range are stored approximately in a binary32 floating point number.

IEEE 754 Binary Formats

The IEEE 754 standard defines four binary floating point formats. Table 10 shows the four formats and some of the programming languages that use them.

Name	Informal Name	Programming Languages
binary16	half precision	
binary32	single precision	Called `float` in C, C++, C#, and Java. Called `Float` in Haskell.
binary64	double precision	Called `double` in C, C++, C#, and Java. Called `Number` in JavaScript. Called `Double` in Haskell. Called `float` in Python. Also, Python `complex` is two binary64 numbers.
binary128	quadruple precision	Sometimes available in C and called `long double`, but this is not guaranteed by the C language.

Table 10: The four IEEE 754 binary floating point formats and some programming languages that use them.

Floating Point Precision

Most real numbers can be only approximated by a binary floating point number which is the disadvantage of floating point numbers. For example, if we use IEEE 754 binary32 format to add 0.1 + 0.2, the sum will not be 0.3 as we expect, but the sum will be 0.300000012. This is because none of the three numbers 0.1, 0.2, or 0.3 can be exactly represented using IEEE 754 binary32 format. All three of them are approximated. Because most real numbers are approximated in any binary floating point format, we may lose accuracy when a computer performs calculations with floating point numbers.

It is important to know how much precision we can expect when the computer performs floating point calculations. Table 11 shows the approximate precision of each of the IEEE 754 binary floating point formats.

Name	sign	Number of Bits exponent	fraction	Approximate Decimal Digits of Precision
binary16	1	5	10	3
binary32	1	8	23	7
binary64	1	11	52	16
binary128	1	15	112	34

Table 11: Approximate precision of four IEEE 754 binary floating point formats.

From Table 11 we learn that if we are writing a program that must store real numbers with eight significant decimal digits, we should use binary64 floating point numbers and not binary16 or binary32. For example, if we write C or Java code to store 4194305.3 as a binary32 number:

```
float x = 4194305.3F;
```

the computer will actually store 4194305.5 because a binary32 number has only 23 bits of precision which is about 7 decimal digits of precision. The computer must approximate the last decimal digit of 4194305.3 as .5. Here is Java code and its output that demonstrates the loss of precision.

Example 9

```
float[] data = {
    4194305.0F, 4194305.1F, 4194305.2F, 4194305.3F,
    4194305.4F, 4194305.5F, 4194305.6F, 4194305.7F,
    4194305.8F, 4194305.9F
};
for (int i = 0;  i < data.length;  ++i) {
    System.out.println(i + " " + data[i]);
}

// Output
0 4194305.0
1 4194305.0
2 4194305.0
3 4194305.5
4 4194305.5
5 4194305.5
6 4194305.5
7 4194305.5
8 4194306.0
9 4194306.0
```

Notice in the output above that the numbers 4194305.1 and 4194305.2 are rounded down to 4194305.0. The numbers 4194305.3, 4194305.4, 4194305.6, and 4194305.7 are rounded to 4194305.5. And the numbers 4194305.8 and 4194305.9 are rounded up to 4194306.0. A binary32 number simply doesn't have enough bits in the significand to store 4194305.3 precisely, so the computer approximates it as 4194305.5.

Floating Point Ranges

Each of the floating point formats has a range of numbers that can be stored which are shown in Table 12.

From Table 12 we learn that if we are writing a program that must store and process numbers that are greater than 3.4×10^{38}, we must use at least binary64 numbers and not binary16 or binary32 numbers.

Name	Approximate Negative Range		Approximate Positive Range	
	most	smallest	smallest	largest
binary16	-6.55×10^4	-7×10^{-8}	7×10^{-8}	6.55×10^4
binary32	-3.40×10^{38}	-1.4×10^{-45}	1.4×10^{-45}	3.40×10^{38}
binary64	-1.79×10^{308}	-4.9×10^{-324}	4.9×10^{-324}	1.79×10^{308}
binary128	-1.18×10^{4932}	-7×10^{-4966}	7×10^{-4966}	1.18×10^{4932}

Table 12: Approximate ranges of four IEEE 754 binary floating point formats.

Many base 10 integers are stored exactly in a floating point number, but other integers cannot be stored exactly and must be approximated when stored in a floating point number. Table 13 lists the range of integers that each IEEE 754 binary format can store exactly. This information is especially interesting when programming in a language like JavaScript, which has only one data type for all numbers. JavaScript uses only IEEE 754 double precision for all numbers, integer and real. This means that in a JavaScript program most integers more negative than -2^{53} and larger than 2^{53} are approximated.

Name	Size	Range	
binary16	2 bytes	$[-2^{11}, 2^{11}]$	$= [-2048,\ 2048]$
binary32	4 bytes	$[-2^{24}, 2^{24}]$	$= [-16,777,216,\ 16,777,216]$
binary64	8 bytes	$[-2^{53}, 2^{53}]$	$= [-9,007,199,254,740,992,\ 9,007,199,254,740,992]$
binary128	16 bytes	$[-2^{113}, 2^{113}]$	$= [-10,384,593,717,069,655,257,060,992,658,440,192,$ $10,384,593,717,069,655,257,060,992,658,440,192]$

Table 13: Ranges of integers that are stored exactly (not approximated) in four IEEE 754 binary floating point formats.

Comparing Floating Point Numbers

Comparing floating point numbers for equality is problematic. This is because most real numbers are approximated when stored as a floating point number. So there is almost always rounding that occurs each time calculations are performed with floating point numbers. Consider the simple example of adding 0.1 ten times as shown in this simple Java code and its output:

```
float f = 0.1f;
float sum = 0;
for (int i = 0;  i < 10;  ++i) {
    sum += f;
}
System.out.println("sum = " + sum);

// Output
sum = 1.0000001
```

Similar code written in C gives a more exact but equally strange output.

```
float f = 0.1f;
float sum = 0;
for (int i = 0;  i < 10;  ++i) {
    sum += f;
}
printf("sum = %.15f\n", sum);

/* Output */
sum = 1.000000014901161
```

Of course, neither answer is correct because the correct answer to 0.1 added ten times is obviously 1. Because of the rounding error that occurs when the computer performs floating point calculations we cannot compare floating point numbers for equality with the simple equality operator (==) that we use for integers. We must compare floating point numbers in a way that returns true when the numbers are close enough to be considered equal. One simple way to compare two floating point numbers is to compare the absolute difference between the two numbers like this:

```
if (Math.abs(f1 - f2) <= epsilon) {
    // f1 and f2 are equal.
}
else {
    // f1 and f2 are not equal.
}
```

But how do we choose the value for *epsilon*? For some applications, we may know the range of values that will be in *f1* and *f2* and will be able to choose a good *epsilon*, but for many applications, we know very little about the range of values that will be in *f1* and *f2*. Perhaps the value of *epsilon* could be calculated from the values of *f1* and *f2*. One possibility is to calculate *epsilon* as a percentage of the larger of *f1* and *f2*. For example:

```java
float epsilon = Math.max(Math.abs(f1), Math.abs(f2)) * 0.01;
if (Math.abs(f1 - f2) <= epsilon) {
    // f1 and f2 are equal.
}
else {
    // f1 and f2 are not equal.
}
```

The previous Java code will compare two floats *f1* and *f2* to see if the distance between them is within 1% of the larger float. Of course, the 1% could be changed to be smaller if we desire. This is a pretty good way to compare floating point numbers. However, computer scientists have known for a long time that comparing floating point numbers for equality is problematic, so they developed some concepts and functions to help.

One concept that can help us compare two floating point numbers is **unit in the last place** which is often abbreviated as **ulp**. An ulp is the unit of least significance within a floating point number. In other words it is the distance from one positive floating point number to the next larger floating point number. We can use the concept of ulp to make floating point comparisons for equality more exact and robust. Java contains two functions in the Math class for computing ulps: Math.ulp(float f) and Math.ulp(double d). Many programming languages that include floating point arithmetic include a function to calculate ulps. Here is Java code to compare two floats for equality by checking if the distance between them is less than or equal to two ulps of the larger float.

```java
float ulp = Math.ulp(Math.max(Math.abs(f1), Math.abs(f2)));
if (Math.abs(f1 - f2) <= ulp * 2) {
    // The distance between f1 and f2 is less than or equal
    // to 2 ulps of the larger of f1 and f2, so they are
    // close enough to be considered equal.
}
else {
    // The distance between f1 and f2 is larger than
    // than 2 ulps of the larger of f1 and f2, so they
    // are considered unequal.
}
```

We could use this code to build a small function that we can use to compare two floating point numbers for equality.

```
public boolean equal(float f1, float f2, int maxULPs) {
    int s1 = (int)Math.signum(f1);
    int s2 = (int)Math.signum(f2);
    boolean equ;
    if (s1 != s2) {
        // The signs of f1 and f2 are different
        // so f1 and f2 are not equal.
        equ = false;
    }
    else if (s1 == 0) {
        // s1 and s2 are both zero which means f1
        // and f2 are both zero so they are equal.
        equ = true;
    }
    else {
        float ulp = Math.ulp(Math.max(Math.abs(f1), Math.abs(f2)));
        equ = Math.abs(f1 - f2) <= ulp * maxULPs;
    }
    return equ;
}
```

This function may seem complex and may run slowly, but if we use simpler and naive techniques for comparing floating point numbers for equality, then we may have faster code but it will return incorrect results for some numbers. What good is fast code if it returns incorrect results?

Chapter Summary

- A base 10 real number can be stored in a computer using a binary integer for the whole part of the real number and a separate binary integer for the fractional part.
- Real numbers stored with the whole and fractional parts separated may consume lots of memory and be slow in calculations.
- Floating point numbers trade precision for smaller memory size and faster computation speed.
- The IEEE 754 standard defines four binary floating point formats: binary16, binary32, binary64, and binary128.
- All four of the IEEE 754 binary formats divide the floating point number into three parts: a sign bit, an exponent, and a fraction.
- binary64 is the most widely used IEEE 754 binary format and can store numbers with approximately 16 decimal digits of precision. It can store numbers as small as 4.9×10^{-324} with only one binary digit of precision and as large as 1.79×10^{308} with 16 decimal digits of precision.
- Comparing floating point numbers for equality is problematic because of the rounding error that occurs when a computer performs floating point arithmetic.
- A reasonable function for comparing floating numbers for equality involves the unit in the last place (ulp) of the larger floating point number.

Review Questions

1. What decimal number is represented by the binary number 01110100.0111? Show your work.
2. Convert the decimal number 109.0875 to a binary number with a whole byte and a fractional nibble. Show your work.
3. Convert the IEEE 754 binary32 number c45a099a to decimal. Show your work. Hint: first convert the binary32 number from hexadecimal to binary, then from binary to decimal using the formula given in the *Converting a Floating Point Number to Decimal* section of this chapter.
4. What IEEE 754 binary floating point format should be used to store the decimal number 74108913.7652? Why?

Really Understand Binary

Appendix
Answers to Review Questions

Chapter 1 Review Questions

1. Count vertically from 0 to 50 inclusive in decimal, binary, and hexadecimal.

Decimal	Binary	Hexadecimal
0	0	0
1	1	1
2	10	2
3	11	3
4	100	4
5	101	5
6	110	6
7	111	7
8	1000	8
9	1001	9
10	1010	a
11	1011	b
12	1100	c
13	1101	d
14	1110	e
15	1111	f
16	10000	10
17	10001	11
18	10010	12
19	10011	13
20	10100	14
21	10101	15
22	10110	16
23	10111	17
24	11000	18
25	11001	19
26	11010	1a
27	11011	1b
28	11100	1c
29	11101	1d

Decimal	Binary	Hexadecimal
30	11110	1e
31	11111	1f
32	100000	20
33	100001	21
34	100010	23
35	100011	23
36	100100	24
37	100101	25
38	100110	26
39	100111	27
40	101000	28
41	101001	29
42	101010	2a
43	101011	2b
44	101100	2c
45	101101	2d
46	101110	2e
47	101111	2f
48	110000	30
49	110001	31
50	110010	32

2. Convert the binary number 0110 1010 to hexadecimal and decimal. Show your work.

Binary   **Hexadecimal**
0110 1010   =   6a

			Binary						**Decimal**
128	**64**	**32**	**16**	**8**	**4**	**2**	**1**		
0	*1*	*1*	*0*	*1*	*0*	*1*	*0*	=	*64*
									32
									8
									2
									106

3. Convert the hexadecimal number 2e to binary and decimal. Show your work.

Hexadecimal   **Binary**
2e   =   0010 1110

			Binary						**Decimal**
128	**64**	**32**	**16**	**8**	**4**	**2**	**1**		
0	*0*	*1*	*0*	*1*	*1*	*1*	*0*	=	*32*
									8
									4
									2
									46

4. Convert the decimal number 123 to binary and hexadecimal. Show your work.

Decimal

				Binary						**Decimal**
		128	**64**	**32**	**16**	**8**	**4**	**2**	**1**	
123	=	*0*	*1*	*1*	*1*	*1*	*0*	*1*	*1*	=	*64*

123
−64
59
−32
27
−16
11
−8
3
−2
1
−1
0

64
32
16
8
2
1
123

Binary   **Hexadecimal**
0111 1011   =   7b

Chapter 2 Review Questions

Perform the following calculations using 8 bit, two's complement, binary arithmetic. Check your answers by converting each binary answer to decimal and comparing it to the expected decimal result. Show your work.

1. 37 + 62

Decimal		Binary								Decimal
		sign	**64**	**32**	**16**	**8**	**4**	**2**	**1**	
37	=	0	0	1	0	0	1	0	1	
+ 62	=	0	0	1	1	1	1	1	0	
sum		0	1	1	0	0	0	1	1	= 64
										32
										2
										1
										99

2. 59 − 29

Decimal		Binary								Decimal
		sign	**64**	**32**	**16**	**8**	**4**	**2**	**1**	
29	=	0	0	0	1	1	1	0	1	
invert		1	1	1	0	0	0	1	0	
+ 1									1	
−29	=	1	1	1	0	0	0	1	1	
+ 59	=	0	0	1	1	1	0	1	1	
sum		0	0	0	1	1	1	1	0	= 16
										8
										4
										2
										30

Really Understand Binary

3. $73 - 113$

Decimal		**Binary**							Decimal
	sign	**64**	**32**	**16**	**8**	**4**	**2**	**1**	
113 =	0	1	1	1	0	0	0	1	
invert	1	0	0	0	1	1	1	0	
+ 1								1	
− 113 =	1	0	0	0	1	1	1	1	
+ 73 =	0	1	0	0	1	0	0	1	
sum	1	1	0	1	1	0	0	0	= −40
sum	1	1	0	1	1	0	0	0	
invert	0	0	1	0	0	1	1	1	
+ 1								1	
	0	0	1	0	1	0	0	0	= 32
									8
									40

4. $-19-42$

Decimal		sign	64	32	16	8	4	2	1		Decimal
19	=	0	0	0	1	0	0	1	1		
invert		1	1	1	0	1	1	0	0		
+ 1									1		
−19	=	1	1	1	0	1	1	0	1		
42	=	0	0	1	0	1	0	1	0		
invert		1	1	0	1	0	1	0	1		
+ 1									1		
−42	=	1	1	0	1	0	1	1	0		
− 19	=	1	1	1	0	1	1	0	1		
− 42	=	1	1	0	1	0	1	1	0		
sum		1	1	0	0	0	0	1	1	=	−61
sum		1	1	0	0	0	0	1	1		
invert		0	0	1	1	1	1	0	0		
+ 1									1		
		0	0	1	1	1	1	0	1	=	32
											16
											8
											4
											1
											61

This is an alternate solution which is possible because $-19-42 = -(19 + 42)$.

Decimal		sign	64	32	16	8	4	2	1		Decimal
19	=	0	0	0	1	0	0	1	1		
42	=	0	0	1	0	1	0	1	0	=	61
sum		0	0	1	1	1	1	0	1		
invert		1	1	0	0	0	0	1	0		
+ 1									1		
answer		1	1	0	0	0	0	1	1	=	−61

Chapter 3 Review Questions

1. Compute 37 ^ 62 in binary. In other words, convert 37 and 62 to binary and combine them using bitwise exclusive or.

Decimal					Binary				
		sign	64	32	16	8	4	2	1
37	=	0	0	1	0	0	1	0	1
62	=	0	0	1	1	1	1	1	0
37 ^ 62	=	0	0	0	1	1	0	1	1

2. Compute 19 | (1 << 3) in binary.

Decimal					Binary				
		sign	64	32	16	8	4	2	1
1	=	0	0	0	0	0	0	0	1
1 << 3	=	0	0	0	0	1	0	0	0
(1 << 3)	=	0	0	0	0	1	0	0	0
19	=	0	0	0	1	0	0	1	1
19 / ~(1 << 3)	=	0	0	0	1	1	0	1	1

3. Compute 59 & ~(1 << 3) in binary.

Decimal					Binary				
		sign	64	32	16	8	4	2	1
1	=	0	0	0	0	0	0	0	1
1 << 3	=	0	0	0	0	1	0	0	0
~(1 << 3)	=	1	1	1	1	0	1	1	1
~(1 << 3)	=	1	1	1	1	0	1	1	1
59	=	0	0	1	1	1	0	1	1
59 & ~(1 << 3)	=	0	0	1	1	0	0	1	1

4.   Compute 58 & (58 − 1) in binary.

Decimal		sign	64	32	16	8	4	2	1
					Binary				
1	=	0	0	0	0	0	0	0	1
invert		1	1	1	1	1	1	1	0
+ 1									1
− 1	=	1	1	1	1	1	1	1	1
− 1	=	1	1	1	1	1	1	1	1
+ 58	=	0	0	1	1	1	0	1	0
58 − 1	=	0	0	1	1	1	0	0	1
58	=	0	0	1	1	1	0	1	0
57	=	0	0	1	1	1	0	0	1
58 & 57	=	0	0	1	1	1	0	0	0

Chapter 4 Review Questions

1. What decimal number is represented by the binary number 01110100.0111? Show your work.

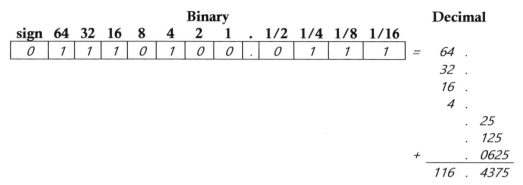

	Binary													**Decimal**
sign	64	32	16	8	4	2	1	.	1/2	1/4	1/8	1/16		
0	1	1	1	0	1	0	0	.	0	1	1	1	=	64 .
														32 .
														16 .
														4 .
														. 25
														. 125
													+	. 0625
														116 . 4375

2. Convert the decimal number 109.3125 to a binary number with a whole byte and a fractional nibble. Show your work.

Decimal			**Binary**												
			sign	64	32	16	8	4	2	1	.	1/2	1/4	1/8	1/16
109 . 3125	=		0	1	1	1	0	1	0	0	.	0	1	0	1

Decimal		
109	.	3125
−64	.	
45	.	3125
−32	.	
13	.	3125
−8	.	
5	.	3125
−4	.	
1	.	3125
−1	.	
0	.	3125
−0	.	25
0	.	0625
−0	.	0625
0	.	0

3. Convert the IEEE 754 binary32 number c45a099a to decimal. Show your work. Hint: first convert the binary32 number from hexadecimal to binary, then from binary to decimal using the formula given in the *Converting a Floating Point Number to Decimal* section of chapter 4.

c45a099a = 1100 0100 0101 1010 0000 1001 1001 1010

sign	exponent								fraction																						
1	1	0	0	0	1	0	0	0	1	0	1	1	0	1	0	0	0	0	0	1	0	0	1	1	0	0	1	1	0	1	0
31	30								23	22																					0

$sign = 1$

$$exponent = 1000\ 1000$$
$$= 128 + 8$$
$$= 136$$

$$fraction = 101\ 1010\ 0000\ 1001\ 1001\ 1010$$
$$= \frac{1}{2} + \frac{1}{8} + \frac{1}{16} + \frac{1}{64} + \frac{1}{4096} + \frac{1}{32768} + \frac{1}{65536} + \frac{1}{524288} + \frac{1}{1048576}$$
$$+ \frac{1}{4194304}$$
$$= \frac{2950349}{4194304}$$
$$= 0.703418016$$

$$value = (-1)^1\ (1 + 0.703418016)\ 2^{136-127}$$
$$= -872.150024$$

4. What IEEE 754 binary floating point format should be used to store the decimal number 74108913.7652? Why?

IEEE 754 binary64 (also called double precision) should be used because the decimal number 74108913.7652 has 12 significant digits and binary32 can store only 7 decimal digits.

Index

IPv4, 39

Java, 29, 30, 52, 60, 64

JavaScript, 62

left shift. *See* bitwise operators

long, 29

long word, 7

multiplicand, 24

multiplication. *See* arithmetic operators

multiplier, 24

negation. *See* arithmetic operators

network mask, 39

nibble, 7, 11

not. *See* bitwise operators

number system, 3

one-time pad, 47

or. *See* bitwise operators

positional number system, 3, 6

product, 24

Python, 30, 60

quotient, 25

range, 26, 62

real number, 51

remainder, 25

right shift. *See* bitwise operators

router, 39

scientific notation, 53

set, 29

short, 29

sign bit, 18, 31, 54

significand, 53, 54

two's complement, 18

ulp, 64

unit in the last place, 64

word, 7

About the Author

Rex A. Barzee is a professor of Computer Information Technology at Brigham Young University – Idaho. He is an inventor of two United States patents and the author of numerous books. He earned a bachelor's and a master's degree in Computer Science from Brigham Young University. Before becoming a professor, he worked in industry for eight years as a software engineer for Southwest Research Institute, Hewlett-Packard Company, Voyant Technologies, and the Utah State University Space Dynamics Laboratory. He worked on a variety of projects including the HP-UX kernel, the HP-UX standard C library, HP-UX OpenGL 3D Graphics Library, full text indexing, image processing, and VoiceXML applications. You can see his full profile at LinkedIn.

Books by the Author

Printed in Poland
by Amazon Fulfillment
Poland Sp. z o.o., Wrocław